CAREERS
IN
THE OUTDOORS

CAREERS IN

Mark
Boesch

THE OUTDOORS

A Sunrise Book

E. P. DUTTON & CO., INC. NEW YORK

1975

Library of Congress Cataloging in Publication Data

Boesch, Mark J 1917-
Careers in the outdoors.

"A Sunrise book."
1. Conservation of natural resources—Vocational guidance.
2. Outdoor recreation—Vocational guidance. I. Title.
S944.B63 1975   333.7'2'023   74-23340

First Edition

10 9 8 7 6 5 4 3 2 1

Published simultaneously in Canada by Clarke, Irwin & Company Limited,
Toronto and Vancouver
ISBN: 0-87690-154-2
Dutton—Sunrise, Inc., a subsidiary of E. P. Dutton & Co., Inc.
Designed by The Etheredges

91738

To Anna Marie

CONTENTS

vii

LIST
OF ILLUSTRATIONS

PREFACE

Increasing numbers of young people are turning to outdoor work for fulfillment and satisfaction in living. This is also true for some who are not so young, but who are fed up with the rat race of making a living in the city.

There is indeed great satisfaction to be found in good, wholesome, useful outdoor work. Whether your interest lies in helping put out a raging forest fire, creating a better habitat for an endangered species of wildlife, helping to stop soil erosion, constructing outdoor recreation facilities, or just writing about and taking pictures of these and related outdoor work activities, you may find a niche in this challenging and truly rewarding field of endeavor.

Reasonably good health and the ability to endure hard physical labor are first requirements for most of the jobs described in this book. You may be city born and bred, and yet adapt well to the outdoor work life. Aptitude is the prime ingredient. Not everyone is willing or able to forsake the ease and comforts of city life for the more rugged outdoor existence. There may be times, sometimes weeks at a stretch, when such work takes you far afield, camping in remote wilderness areas, often relying on your own abilities and resources to maintain yourself.

For those who have the calling to live and work in the outdoors, roughing it is one of the deep satisfactions that come with the life. But an even greater satisfaction is the knowledge that you are accomplishing worthwhile work, work that becomes increasingly important as we recognize man's often harmful effects on the environment.

In earlier times, outdoor work was much simpler than it is today. About all it required was the desire and the brawn to work hard. Today, like most other aspects of living, outdoor jobs have become more complicated and specialized. Special training is usually required if you are to qualify for a meaningful job. This training is readily available. Besides the many professional schools around the country, there are today in states as far removed as New York and Montana special two-year schools of technology that teach many of the skills that go with an outdoor career. I shall mention examples of these throughout the book, and a complete listing is given in Appendix A.

But attendance at one of these schools is not necessary for a job in the outdoors. Public land management agencies as well as private employers are currently giving added attention to on-the-job training. And often they send a promising employee to a specialized school to round out his education. The point to keep in mind is, the better training you have, the better chance you have for advancement in the outdoor career you choose to follow.

Another way of beginning an outdoor work career, and one I recommend to many young people, is enlistment in a work program such as the Youth Conservation Corps. The YCC is modeled on the famed Civilian Conservation Corps of the 1930s. In

Mark Boesch in the Sylvania Recreation Area, Ottawa National Forest. (*Richard Bauer*, Milwaukee Journal)

its fourth year at this writing, the YCC has been greatly expanded owing to the success it enjoyed during its three trial years.

The YCC enables young men and women from the ages of fifteen to nineteen to enroll for approximately eight weeks during the summer in useful conservation work on such public lands as the national forests and the national parks. During this time you will be paid for your work, and in many cases you will be doing the same work and even living under much the same conditions as you would in a regular outdoor work career. After eight weeks in the YCC, you should know if you have the aptitude for outdoor work.

Although many occupations involve working outdoors—farming, ranching, road building—this book deals with outdoor jobs related to the conservation of natural resources. Many different types of jobs are available in this field, and this book will guide you in the kind of training you need to qualify and tell you where to get that training and how to land one of these jobs.

These jobs used to be low paid. But that situation is changing as the demand for good, skilled outdoor workers continues to increase. Salary should not, however, be your main consideration. You can generally make more money in a skilled trade or profession in the cities.

This book is based on my many years of experience with the U.S. Forest Service, during which time I also often worked with and observed the work of other public conservation agencies and private organizations. Many friends have been kind enough to supply me with current information on careers in their agencies and organizations. These people are too numerous to cite here, but they know who they are, and they know I appreciate their help. Some of them I mention in the text as models for various careers.

One final word—read all the book, not just the chapter or chapters you are particularly interested in. It is important to get the whole picture. All these jobs are interrelated.

CAREERS
IN
THE OUTDOORS

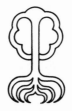

1: YOUR CAREER IN FORESTRY AND TIMBER MANAGEMENT

Everyone has to become something of a specialist these days. If you can learn the skills and gain experience in one particular kind of work, you have an advantage that will help you get ahead. This is as true in the outdoor field as in any other.

But no matter how good a specialist you become, you should also be something of a generalist. You must understand other jobs that are related to yours. Such understanding will help you not only to do your own particular job better, but also to advance to a more responsible position, supervising workers both in your own specialty and outside it.

With this in mind, I decided to begin with careers in timber management because that specialty is associated with the science of forestry, and forestry is a good general subject as well as an

1

important basic discipline in the field of natural resource conservation.

WHAT IS NATURAL RESOURCE CONSERVATION?

The idea of natural resource conservation originated with Gifford Pinchot, founder and first chief of the U.S. Forest Service and the man who got the conservation movement going in America back at the turn of this century. Pinchot spent a long lifetime as an active conservationist, and just before his death in 1946 he finished a definitive book on the movement he started. The book, called *Breaking New Ground,* should be required reading for all who wish to work in the conservation field. Pinchot wrote:

> *Conservation means the wise use of the earth and its resources for the lasting good of men. Conservation is the foresighted utilization, preservation, and/or renewal of forests, waters, lands, and minerals, for the greatest good of the greatest number for the longest time.*

Many have tried, but I think none has succeeded in writing a better definition of conservation. And conservation of natural resources, the wise use of them, is as important today as it ever has been.

WHAT IS FORESTRY?

Forestry deals with the utilization and protection of forestlands so that they will continue to yield raw materials and an increasing number of forest products for the benefit of all the people. Forestry in its strictest sense deals with the management of a renewable natural resource known as timber. But in its broadest sense, forestry deals with all the natural resources found in a forested area—such basics, for example, as water, wildlife, and forage.

Two young men in the Job Corps conservation program.

We begin to understand why Pinchot, as chief forester of the U.S. Forest Service, pioneered multiple-use management of all natural resources found on a forested area, rather than just timber alone. Pinchot was an ecologist. He knew that a forest was a community of living things and must be treated as such. For the best health of man and his environment, that living community must be kept in balance and harmony.

The science of forestry is, then, the science of forest management. Note that I did not say timber management. It is important to make the distinction that forestry deals with much more than timber alone.

WORKING IN FORESTRY

Careers in forestry are available at several levels. Professional forester is the top job. Nonprofessional workers are classed as timber management technicians. These people do all sorts of work: they supervise the sale of timber from Forest Service land, work at timber stand improvement, plant trees, and dispose of slash. Such jobs are closely related, and the lower level, hard labor jobs are particularly valuable as training experiences to start the worker on a career in the forests and woodlands.

PROFESSIONAL FORESTER

Forest management is the job of the professional forester. Timber management is an important part of that job, but it's not the forester's only concern. He may also be called upon to be a wildlife manager, a soil and water manager, a range manager, an engineer, a forest fire manager, or a recreation manager. To be an effective administrator of a forested area, he needs to know a good deal about all these other disciplines.

The forester is also greatly concerned with research. Man has not learned enough about the dynamics of forest management. Research reveals new truths about the living communities in a forest, how they relate to one another, and how best to keep them in healthy balance. Forestry research also reveals the best ways to get the maximum use out of forest products. For example, research has given us some 5,000 useful products from wood for our modern civilization, thanks largely to the development of wood chemistry. That is why many leading colleges of forestry offer courses in wood chemistry. Other courses taught at these colleges are forest management; wood science, technology, and utilization; forest products marketing and merchandising; building engineering and construction; pulp and paper technology; and subjects allied to these, such as biology, botany, silviculture, mathematics, and chemistry.

A forester must also possess an aptitude for human relations and business management. Today the forester must increasingly deal with the public in his decision making and must increasingly make management decisions that are as sound in a business way as they are ecologically.

Obviously, then, a forester must gain a liberal as well as a technical education to succeed. A college degree is essential. Appendix B of this book lists the colleges and universities that offer professional education programs for the degree of forester.

Jim Greene, Forester

My friend Jim Greene decided on a professional forestry career. The remarkable thing about this is that Jim's father and grandfather were West Point graduates and career army officers. It was generally assumed that Jim would himself have a military career. But when young he came to love the outdoors, and he thought nothing could be finer than making his living working outdoors. He got a taste of this fighting forest fires in Arkansas. And so he put himself through forestry school.

Today Jim Greene is in charge of the forestry program for an important forested county. He works for a state forestry department administering a cooperative state and federal program, giving advice to private landowners on the management of their timberlands. It is important work, assuring the owners of a profit from their timberlands and assuring a future timber supply for the country. And for Jim it is enjoyable work. Though he maintains an office in the county seat, he is not often in that office. He is most apt to be found out on some timbered tract, going over it with the owner, deciding on the best management policies.

Laura Smith, Forester

The field is not confined to men. Recently, in the Northwest, a bad tussock moth epidemic struck. The Douglas fir tussock moth has been responsible for killing thousands of acres of this most valuable species of timber in years past. Laura Smith, a graduate of the University of Washington in forest ecology, and today a forester employed by the Idaho Department of Public Lands, supervised one of several field sampling crews whose duty was to determine dates of egg hatch and to measure prespray and postspray tussock moth populations. It was Laura Smith who discovered the first incidence of tussock moth egg hatching. She appears to be another young forester launched on a successful career.

TIMBER MANAGEMENT TECHNICIAN

Not everyone has the means or inclination to go to a four-year college. For these people, too, there is a place in forestry. In fact, today there is a greater need for good timber management technicians than for professional foresters. That is because public agencies dealing with natural resource conservation, as well as private companies practicing timber management, find they need about five technicians for every professional on their payrolls.

Timber management technicians—also called forestry technicians—are increasingly taking over the jobs and duties once considered the province of professional foresters alone. One reason for this is that timber management has become a specific occupation that calls for well-trained specialists. Another reason is that timber management involves practical skills rather than theoretical knowledge. This does not mean, however, that the timber management technician need be a narrow specialist. As I pointed out in the beginning of this chapter, the more general knowledge a specialist acquires, the better specialist he becomes.

General Educational Requirements

Essentially, what you need to be a good timber management technician are good basic woodsman's skills. You must love the woods and want to work out in them in all kinds of weather. You must be in good physical condition. You must know how to use the woodsman's tools—the ax, power saw, compass, and map.

You can learn to use these tools and gain other necessary skills on the job, but you will be doing yourself and your future employer a favor if you begin learning something about them before you embark on your career of timber management technician. Today many schools offer technical and vocational training in timber management (see Appendix A).

These schools teach you such important subjects as forest

technology, forest products technology, timber harvesting technology, and pulp and paper technology. Most offer a two-year course for a diploma or certificate. Some offer a one-year course for more advanced students or those who can combine practical experience with a high school diploma or its equivalent.

Advantages and Disadvantages

What are the advantages and disadvantages of becoming a timber management technician rather than a professional forester? Let's discuss the disadvantages first.

As a timber management technician your advancement in a forestry organization may be limited. You will be limited in the kinds of work you are qualified to do. Hence, you will have to settle for less pay than the professional forester gets.

For many people these disadvantages weigh heavily against being a technician rather than a full-fledged professional. For others being a technician has many more advantages than disadvantages.

A technician can find employment almost immediately, and that is certainly a decided advantage. As I write this, newly graduated foresters are having a difficult time finding jobs, including jobs with the U.S. Forest Service, the largest employer of foresters in the world. I know one graduate forester, a bright young man, who had to settle for a job as a brush piler in a national forest his first year out of school. And he got that because he had the courage and determination to leave home and go where such laboring jobs could be found.

Located in this same region where the young graduate forester failed to find professional forestry work is a leading vocational school, offering both one-year and two-year technical courses in timber management. The director of the school told me he is able to place immediately about 75 percent of his graduates in timber management jobs. The percentage could be greater, he assured me, but many who take the course decide to go into other kinds of work or even on to college to become forestry professionals.

The latter career route should not be overlooked. You don't have to remain a timber management technician all your career, just because you went to a technical school or began working as a technician in the woods. Many of these schools offer a preprofessional program, preparing the student to continue on to a degree in forestry.

Another advantage to becoming a technician rather than a forestry professional is that the technician does more of his work outdoors. Many people, women as well as men, would much rather work outdoors than in an office. In my many years with the U.S. Forest Service, and when I was stationed in a regional headquarters in a large city, I heard many professionals moan that they could no longer spend as much time in the woods as they did earlier in their careers. Being stuck indoors is often the price of success for a professional forester in an agency such as the Forest Service. He becomes more an administrator than an outdoor worker. That is fine for those who like the position, responsibility, and higher salary that go with such success. But for many others it is a distinct disadvantage.

The timber management technician, no matter how skilled or experienced he becomes, continues to spend much of his time out in the woods, because that is where the timber is and timber is what his job is all about. He may make less money than the successful forestry professional, but his salary generally goes farther than does the professional's. That's because he is less apt to be transferred from one post to another. The timber management technician tends to stay put. This enables him to become well acquainted with the country he works in. He can sink his roots deep in country he loves. He can make a good home for himself there, have time to enjoy it, and even make it a good investment for the future. This happens most often in a small town, or perhaps even out in the country, where living costs are much less than in the city.

At the same time, the gap in pay between the skilled technician and the competent professional is steadily narrowing. I can remember the time in the Forest Service when what was then called a skilled practical worker could scarcely ever rise above the GS-7 grade level.* This would be equivalent in pay to about the lowest ranking fireman or policeman in a big city. Most professional foresters reached that grade after only a year

* See Appendix D: Government Pay Scales.

A timber management specialist in the Forest Service uses an increment borer to determine timber growth rate.

of experience, and some even started at that grade. Now the GS-7 grade is common for technicians in the Forest Service. Technicians start at the GS-5 grade, many make GS-9, and some rise as high as GS-12. This means they can earn more than $20,000 a year, a higher salary than many professional foresters make. Even as a GS-7, a technician can get into the five-figure pay bracket and enjoy the same fringe benefits of retirement, annual and sick leave, health and hospitalization insurance that the professional has.

Dan, a Timber Management Technician

Shortly after I talked with the director of the vocational school referred to above, I interviewed Dan, one of that school's graduates, at the suggestion of the forester in charge of a leading state forestry program. This important state administrator, though a professional forester himself, wanted me to see how important he considers the timber management technician in his organization. His view is echoed by many other forestry administrators.

Dan graduated from the technical college in 1971. He was then about twenty-four, and he told me the main reason he had chosen the technical school rather than a regular four-year college was that after high school he had gone into military service and then had married. The GI bill paid for his schooling, but barely met his expenses as a family man. He wanted to go to work as soon as possible in the career he had chosen—forestry. He loved the outdoors and the woods.

Dan, who was certainly bright enough to have gone to college, did a wise thing when he graduated from the technical school. He wrote letters of application to a number of organizations that hired foresters, stating his background and schooling. He got several offers of immediate employment, and at good starting pay. Two state forestry departments offered work that appealed to him. He decided on one of these and started at a salary of $6,000 a year.

Dan was given a variety of interesting jobs during the years he worked for the state forestry department. He worked as a timber management assistant during the winter, then became a fire dispatcher during the summer when there were forest fires to fight. And he was rewarded with several raises while he learned the skills that are part of his job.

When I interviewed Dan, he was attending a week-long special training school in his department's headquarters city. He had been in the organization less than three years, had risen to an annual salary of $9,000, and had become an assistant ranger on an important state forest. His fringe benefits included a nice family-size house to live in, rent free, as well as state civil service protection and benefits.

Thus, in less than three years Dan had risen $3,000 in salary and was doing work he loved in country he loved. And the director has assured me there is no limit to how far Dan can go in his organization. Dan knows that, and his morale could not be higher.

Forest Service Timber Sales

There is good reason for the Forest Service of the U.S. Department of Agriculture to be the largest single employer of foresters in the country. Besides having 187 million acres of forestland in 155 national forests to manage, this largest agency in the Department of Agriculture has the responsibility of leading and coordinating forestry activities in the United States. It is a leader in forestry research, having a number of experimental forests and a world-renowned wood products laboratory in Madison, Wisconsin. The Forest Service also manages a number of national grasslands and conducts research in range management.

For many years the Forest Service was chiefly a caretaker organization. It was responsible for preserving the national forests and protecting them from exploitation. Fire control was a big part of the job in those days, and it was the U.S. Forest Service that pioneered effective forest fire control in America. Protection of the national forests also involved building trails, roads, bridges, and other improvements. These things are still important, but since about the time of World War II, the increasing demand for timber products has made timber management an increasingly important aspect of Forest Service responsibility.

The national forests are public lands—hence are owned by all the people. That means timber on the national forests is for all the people to benefit from. Sale of timber from the national forests is important not only to help the country meet its needs for timber products, but also to keep these timberlands healthy. Properly done, timber cutting is beneficial for a forest. By cutting overmature, often diseased trees, and replacing them with younger, more vigorous stock, you improve a forest stand, making it what the foresters call "thrifty," meaning a forest that is healthy and producing vigorously.

A lot of planning goes into making a timber sale. Foresters and technicians look over the country on the ground. The tracts to be sold are drawn on a map. The timber sale boundary is marked, roads are surveyed in, the volume of timber by species is estimated, and a timber sale contract is drawn up specifying how the sale is to be conducted—operating procedures. Then the sale is opened for bidding by private logging companies. Timber sales may be as small as several hundred thousand board feet (it takes about 10,000 board feet to build the average two-bedroom house), or they may be millions of board feet in size. They average around 2 million board feet on most national forests.

After the sale is awarded to the highest bidder, the work of the foresters and technicians does not cease. The sale then has to be supervised by them, to make sure the contracting logging company lives up to contract specifications. This is important, for much harm can be done to the land if timber harvesting is not carried out correctly.

I need only open a catalog from any of the technical schools around the country to see why technicians are taking over many of these timber sale jobs that foresters alone were once assigned. In the catalog are listed courses in the following subjects: orientation to forestry, elementary surveying, advanced surveying, technical drawing, road location, road design and staking, forest

A forester inspecting a timber sale.

ecology and silviculture, insect and disease control, forest measurements, forest products, soils, forestry tools, photo interpretation, marketing and economics, forest economics, forest policy and laws, mathematics, supervision and foremanship, and timber harvesting.

All these courses are designed to give the student the knowledge necessary to enable him to do a creditable job as timber management technician, including planning and supervising a Forest Service timber sale. Of course, besides the usual classroom and laboratory work, much of the student's time is spent out in the forest, seeing with his own eyes what he has been taught indoors. And many students supplement their studies with part-time work for the Forest Service or other timber management agencies, gaining on-the-job experience along with their schooling. Some schools place students in such part-time jobs as a portion of their school curriculum. For example, Southeastern Illinois College in Harrisburg, Illinois, has sent students as far away as the Lolo National Forest in Montana to work during the summer months.

Champ Hannon, Timber Sales Technician

I learned some of the skills and techniques of timber sale work from the late Champ Hannon, who for many years did this work on the Bitterroot National Forest in Montana. Champ had been a district ranger for a time too, but his first love was timber work, and he became a staff man supervising timber sale preparation. This enabled him to spend most of his time in the woods, which he dearly loved. And his greatest joy was to give good care to those woods. The results showed it. His sales were always carefully prepared and well supervised. When the logger was through with them, the tracts were much improved, the timber taken out that should have been taken out, the rest left in a much thriftier condition. When Champ died after a good and long life, the local newspaper eulogized him for his great contribution to good forestry conservation.

Timber Stand Improvement

TSI is what the foresters call timber stand improvement. There is no more important activity to keep a forest healthy and growing vigorously. Quite often it is done following timber harvest, and then it is referred to as sale area betterment (SAB).

Timber stand improvement includes thinning the forest, removing less desirable trees so that more desirable ones will have adequate room for growth and moisture, pruning the residual trees so they will produce more volume of sound board feet of timber, and practicing sanitation measures both to ward off attacks by insects and disease and to make the trees less susceptible to forest fire damage. A good forester gives as much care and concern to a working forest as a farmer gives to his crops in the field. That is what timber stand improvement is all about.

For anyone who loves the outdoors and being out in the woods, this can be among the most enjoyable of jobs. I recall with pleasure my own days doing this work on a large national forest. Since most timber stand improvement work still must be done by hand, it creates a continuous demand for skilled woodsmen—people who know something about silviculture (the study and cultivation of trees for timber) and who know how to use the tools of the trade—the power saw, ax, and pruning saw.

Those who do timber stand improvement work combine it with other duties. They may plant trees, as described below, they may fight fires during the forest fire season, they may do brush disposal work, they may even advance to timber sales administration work. Such was the case with my friend Bud Dorgan.

Bud Dorgan, Timber Management Technician

Bud started on a district doing general labor and fighting forest fires. He became district fire dispatcher during fire season and did timber stand improvement and sale area betterment work during the winter. He even worked in the Job Corps program for a time, helping disadvantaged young men to learn outdoor work skills. Today he is principal timber management technician on an important ranger district, drawing a good salary for timber sales administration work.

Tree Planting

Closely associated with timber stand improvement is tree planting. In many forested areas natural reproduction is not sufficient to restock the land. That is one reason for tree planting.

A shelterbelt planting of cedar trees on the Great Plains. (*U.S. Forest Service*)

Another reason is that some logging practices remove all the trees from a particular area, and the area is then replanted. Still another reason can be natural disaster—devastating fire, insect, or disease attack that wipes out all trees in a forested area.

Hundreds of millions of nursery-grown seedlings are planted every year on forested areas throughout the country—many kinds of trees in many kinds of areas, including places, such as the Great Plains, where trees were not common before. So great has been the intensity of tree planting in Nebraska that that state now has a national forest entirely planted by man!

Much of the planting is, however, done in the South, for there trees grow so fast that seedlings can attain pulpwood size in not much more than ten years, and the pulp industry is very important in southern forestry.

Tree planting has also been important in the Midwest. There, in thirty years or so, over a billion trees were planted on over a million acres of national forestland. Much of this land had once been badly exploited by timber harvesters. States and private landowners have planted additional millions of trees.

Many of these planted areas are now producing sawlogs as well as pulpwood.

Tree planting is widespread in the northeastern states too, where the pulp industry is also important. And even in the heavily forested northwestern United States, tree planting is a necessary activity. Douglas fir, which grows there so magnificently, is today our most important lumber tree. But because the Douglas fir requires much sunlight for best growth, the timber harvesting method known as clear-cutting has been adopted in these coastal forests. The opened-up tracts are re-planted with Douglas fir seedlings, which are then able to win out in competition with hemlock, a shade-loving, inferior species of timber.

Much labor is required in tree planting, both in nursery work and in the actual planting of the trees in the forest, even though modern tools such as mechanized tree planters are used where possible. One of the easiest ways to break into timber management work is to get a tree planting job. There are two times of the year when this is possible—spring and fall. It is hard work, and requires a strong back, but women are as good at it as men.

Pay for tree planting is comparable to pay for other labor jobs. The rate is usually at least $3 an hour, often $4 an hour or more (depending quite a bit on what part of the country you're in). You can find such work in one of the government forest management agencies or in the private sector with one of the large timberland owners or with a contractor who does tree planting on other people's land.

Timber planting obviously is temporary work, but it can be a good way of getting started in an outdoor career. I know many who did start that way.

Slash Disposal

Slash is the debris left after timber harvest, that is, the smaller limbs and unsalable trees. If this debris remains heaped up or strewn about the woods, it becomes a fire hazard. Some of the worst forest fires in our history were fed by slashings left after timber cutting. Hence it is important to get rid of as much slash on a timber sale area as possible.

All this work used to be done by hand, but more and more it is now done by machines, particularly bulldozers. The machines heap the slash into piles; then, under careful supervision, it is burned. In some places, particularly in scenic areas and along roads where the fire hazard is greater, slash is still hand piled for burning.

Another and even better way to dispose of slash is called lopping and scattering. This requires hand labor by people skilled with axes and power saws. They go into an area that has been logged, lop off the limbs of the small trees and trash timber that have been left, and spread them out over the forest floor. This helps to reduce fire hazard because it gets the foliage down close to the ground, where it soon deteriorates. And the deteriorated foliage returns vital nutrients to the soil.

Many jobs of this type are available in both public and

Working in a tree nursery. (*U.S. Forest Service*)

private timber management organizations. They are laboring jobs, paying about the same as tree planting. They are important for the beginning worker because they help him learn to use the tools of his trade and acquaint him with basic forestry principles.

EMPLOYMENT OPPORTUNITIES

THE FOREST SERVICE

The Forest Service of the U.S. Department of Agriculture is the largest single employer of foresters, forestry aids, and technicians in the country. It has over 20,000 permanent employees.

The best way to start work with the Forest Service (as well as other such land management agencies) is by accepting part-time employment during the summer months, perhaps while you are still in school, though in most cases you must have attained the age of eighteen.

Forestry aids on the national forests work at a variety of productive tasks that help both the technician and the professional forester. Some of these tasks are scaling logs; marking trees and collecting and recording such data as tree heights, tree

Using a modern tree planter to regenerate cutover forestland.

diameters, and tree mortality; installing, maintaining, and recording data collected from rain gauges, stream flow recorders, and soil moisture measuring instruments on simple watershed improvement projects. Forestry aids also serve as forest fire fighters during periods of high fire danger.

As a part-time summer employee you can also become a forest worker or laborer, doing some of the jobs discussed above.

The pay is not bad for these jobs. The lowest starting classification is GS-1, and starting pay for that level is about $204 for each two weeks of employment. But most forest aids rate the GS-3 classification, and that pays about $260 for each two weeks of work. Often you can work extra hours at emergency duties, such as forest fire fighting, and be paid extra for this. Not to be overlooked is the fact that often you are stationed some distance from town, at a remote ranger station or woods camp, and in such cases food and lodging are furnished at nominal cost. All things considered, it is a good way to spend the summer, learning while you are earning.

Wage labor rates, which do not come under the general

schedules of government employment, are comparable to equivalent GS rates, but are also based on equivalent wage rates in the part of the country concerned. For example, on a national forest in the South a laborer might make $2.62 per hour, while on a national forest in Montana he would make $2.98 per hour. The pay is based on a cost-of-living index as well as prevailing local wage rates.

The Forest Service furnishes the tools and safety equipment you need to do your work, but you are expected to furnish your own work clothes, including heavy work boots, gloves, and jackets.

Many summer jobs with the Forest Service do not require a written examination. If you qualify and wish to be considered for employment, submit an application to the appropriate regional or national forest office. The locations of these are listed in Appendix D. Submit your application between January 1 and February 15 of any year. Application forms (Standard Form 171) are available at any local post office or Civil Service Commission office.

Competition for Forest Service summer jobs is understandably keen. To enhance your opportunities for summer employment with this and other government agencies, you are well advised to take the examination given by the Civil Service Commission. As vacancies occur for jobs covered by this examination, the Civil Service Commission refers names from the top of the list of eligibles. See Appendix E for information on how to apply for a civil service examination.

THE TENNESSEE VALLEY AUTHORITY

The Tennessee Valley Authority is another source of jobs for foresters, forestry aids, and technicians.

The Tennessee River watershed is a 40,910-square-mile area encompassing parts of seven states. When the TVA was created in 1933, it was given the task of helping this region to put its natural resources to work for all the people. The assignment was difficult, for at that time the valley's average income was less than half the national average, and America was in the throes of economic depression. Natural resources in this part of the country had been badly exploited. People had lost hope and were discouraged.

The TVA went to work. A system of dams was built to harness the Tennessee River to provide flood control, navigation facilities, and cheap electrical power. An idle and obsolete government munitions plant was turned into a national fertilizer development center. Reforestation, forest management, and forest fire control practices were commenced to rebuild depleted woodlands.

The results are truly outstanding. Today the per capita income in the Tennessee Valley is seventeen times what it was in 1933. Four times as many people have jobs in industry. Farming is more efficient and therefore more profitable. And the TVA has itself become an important employer, paying good wages and salaries.

Forestry has been an integral part of the unified development of the Tennessee Valley. Today more than 1.2 million acres of the valley have been reforested. More than half of the total area is covered by forest. Erosion has been controlled, forest fire losses cut to a fraction of former amounts, and wildlife populations increased. The region's forests contain nearly twice as much timber as they did forty years ago, and they are growing three times as much wood as is now being harvested.

But the job is not done. It has, in fact, only begun. Forestry objectives today are more complex than those of the past. As on the national forests, the goal now is to combine maximum watershed protection, scenic beauty, and recreation benefits of forests with a healthy economic contribution in terms of forest products and jobs. Research is under way to improve the quantity and quality of the region's wood supply, to help meet future demands for lumber, furniture, and paper—important wood products in this region.

All this means that jobs in timber management continue to

be available in the TVA area—in the organization itself, in state and other agencies, and in private industry.

The TVA plants a lot of trees. The Pine Tree Branch Watershed near Lexington, Tennessee, is a good example. This is a small 88-acre demonstration area set up to show what can be done to restore forestland that has been badly abused. Years of farming had left the area riddled with gullies, erosion carried away an average of twenty-four tons of soil a year from each acre of land, and the rush of water off the hillsides after each storm fed frequent downstream floods.

After careful measurement of soil loss and stream flow for comparison with later results, the TVA planted the entire watershed in pine seedlings. Erosion control measures such as check dams in gullies were used in addition to providing protection from fire and grazing. Within five years soil loss was dramatically reduced. After fifteen years erosion was virtually stopped, and the runoff from a rainstorm flowed out over days instead of minutes.

Careful tree harvesting is also being done by the TVA to show private landowners that reforestation can provide additional income. Pine Tree Branch, and dozens of other demonstration projects carried out across the Tennessee Valley, with the guidance of TVA foresters, have shown landowners that reforestation benefits both land and owner.

Today the TVA administers a forestry development program designed for watershed protection and timber production, primarily through educational and demonstration activities. While much of this calls for expert work by well-educated foresters, the foresters must be assisted by technicians and workers. Appendix D tells how to apply for a job with the TVA.

THE BUREAU OF LAND MANAGEMENT

The Bureau of Land Management of the U.S. Department of the Interior hires people for timber management work. The BLM administers 464 million acres of public land, of which approximately 149 million acres are forest and woodlands in the western states, including Alaska. The BLM employs approximately 540 professional foresters and many more lower level forestry workers. It describes its forest management program as "youthful, dynamic, and expanding."

Like the national forests, the BLM forests are managed on a multiple-use basis. BLM employees thus become experienced not only in timber management but also in such closely related activities as watershed management, mineral resources, outdoor recreation, land classification, and range management.

The nature of the forestry work depends on where the employee is stationed. For example, the BLM has extensive forestlands in the Douglas fir region of western Oregon. Principal jobs there are in timber sales, including road location, surveying, cruising timber to estimate volumes, marking cutting lines, appraising, and sale administration. Technicians and foresters work up plans for logging, slash disposal, reforestation, and rehabilitation, and oversee the carrying out of these and other silvicultural practices.

Forestry positions and duties are similar outside the Douglas fir region, but there are some variations for specific forest types and species.

Not all forestry positions are related solely to the timber sale program. Many employees are engaged in inventory programs, commercial and precommercial thinnings, and forest protection activities. See Appendix D for further information on jobs with the BLM.

THE SOIL CONSERVATION SERVICE

The Soil Conservation Service in the U.S. Department of Agriculture hires a large number of forestry workers for what it calls woodland conservation work. The SCS is primarily an advisory and educational agency. It manages no land of its own.

The woodland conservationists in the SCS give technical

guidance, training, and other assistance in woodland conservation to SCS employees. They develop technical standards in forestry in collaboration with state forestry agencies. They interpret forestry techniques and experimental data for field use. And they help evaluate soil-tree relations and determine woodland conservation practices in relation to specific soil and site conditions. See Appendix D for more employment information concerning the SCS.

THE FISH AND WILDLIFE SERVICE

The Fish and Wildlife Service in the U.S. Department of the Interior hires a good number of foresters, forestry technicians, aids, and workers. It manages over 300 national wildlife refuges in various parts of the country, and their number continues to grow. Many of these refuges have timberlands that need to be managed. See Appendix D for information about jobs with the Fish and Wildlife Service.

OTHER FEDERAL AGENCIES

A number of other federal agencies hire timber management specialists. In the U.S. Department of Agriculture, the Agricultural Stabilization and Conservation Service administers such forest conservation programs as the rural environmental conservation program, the conservation reserve program of the soil bank, and the Appalachian land stabilization and conservation program.

The Extension Service of the agriculture department hires agents in nearly all counties. County agents must be trained in forestry as well as other natural resource matters.

The U.S. Army Corps of Engineers manages forestland and must have timber management specialists in its employ. The same is true of the Department of the Air Force and the Department of the Navy.

The Bureau of Indian Affairs of the U.S. Department of the Interior serves as a source of technical and financial aid to the various Indian tribes. Included is aid in forest management, and therefore foresters as well as technicians are hired by the agency.

The National Park Service of the Department of the Interior hires many timber management specialists to preserve and protect the thousands of acres of timberland in the parks.

The Environmental Protection Agency, established in 1969 to administer the Environmental Policy Act, has the responsibility for setting and enforcing environmental standards; conducting research on the causes, effects, and control of environmental problems; and assisting state and local governments in these matters. Forestry is much involved, and the agency employs many timber management specialists.

Appendix D supplies information about applying for jobs with these agencies.

STATE ORGANIZATIONS

State forest organizations came into being after forestry became a recognized science in the United States. Many developed during the depression years of the 1930s, when it was recognized that much rehabilitation work was necessary to make the state forestlands healthy again.

After World War II increasing demands for timber focused attention on cutting timber in state forests, as in national forests. This caused the state forest organizations to expand greatly. Many jobs were created, and the expansion has not yet ceased.

Your chances for employment on a state forest are very good, particularly if you reside in the state where the forest is located, though that is not a requirement for most of the professional and even the technician jobs. Part-time as well as full-time jobs are available.

Pay used to be less than in federal agencies, but that has changed in recent years. Dan, whose career was described earlier, has done as well financially working for a state forest organization as he would have in federal employment. And I think that is going to become more and more the case.

You don't have to go to the Far West, the Far North, or the Deep South to gain good employment in timber management. There may be a state forest organization offering excellent employment opportunities right in your own home state. To find out, inquire at the state forest organization's headquarters or a branch office.

Timber management jobs in private industry, though discussed here last, are by no means least. While the U.S. Forest Service is the largest single employer of timber management workers, private industry as a whole is the largest overall employer, hiring as many as one third of all the foresters in the United States and the same proportion of timber management technicians and workers.

Some of the largest timber companies hire thousands of people for woods work. These companies own many thousands of acres of timberland and they do all the types of work done on the national forests, including timber stand improvement and timber planting as well as actual timber harvesting. Like the government forester, the industry forester's job is growing trees forever and practicing sustained-yield forestry on the company's holdings.

The forest products industry is one of the largest employers of all types in the United States. According to the National Forest Products Association, "statistics for April 1972 show that nationwide employment in the lumber and wood products, furniture and fixtures, and pulp and paper segments of the forest industry exceeded 1.75 million people, with an annual payroll of over $12.5 billion."

The kind of jobs available in timber management in private industry, besides those already described in connection with the Forest Service, include work associated with actual timber har-

Working in the pulpwood industry in Wisconsin. (*U.S. Forest Service*)

vesting—pulpwood cutting and hauling, sawing in the woods, running bulldozers and other types of heavy equipment, and hauling the logs to the mill. This is hard work, and it can be dangerous work. There was good reason for the old-time lumberjack to be the tough man he was. But today's conditions are greatly improved. Safety is a foremost consideration, and there are many safer and better tools as well as safer means to harvest and haul the timber. Still, timber harvesting remains hard and often dangerous work. It requires strength and skill. That's why it pays well.

Young, inexperienced workers can often start in jobs in the

private timber management industry at wages of $4 an hour or better, and with many of the same fringe benefits that federal civil service workers have. Advancement can also be rapid, and as you gain the necessary skills and know-how you can soon double your starting salary.

If you want the best kind of job in private timber management work, you should prepare yourself well. That means either going to college and becoming a forester, or going to one of the technical schools that teach timber management skills. Companies often offer part-time jobs to students to help them meet their educational expenses.

For further information write:

National Forest Products Association
1619 Massachusetts Avenue N.W.
Washington, D.C. 20036

Harold Oliff, Lumberjack

Harold Oliff is an example of a successful modern lumberjack. He was raised on a farm in Virginia, and like so many others, emigrated to the city to seek better economic opportunities. But though he made good wages in the electronics industry, he wanted to get back outdoors. His wife felt the same way, so they headed west.

In Wyoming the logging industry attracted Oliff because it offered a chance to work in the woods, and it seemed to pay good wages. Though he lacked formal schooling beyond the high school level, Harold Oliff had several other things going for him. On the farm he'd had to tinker with machinery, and he had an aptitude for mechanical work. He thus came to understand power saws and other equipment used in the woods. He was a strong man and was not afraid of hard work. He was quick to learn and adapted rapidly to this new life style. These characteristics made him a success.

For a time Harold Oliff did most of the rudimentary jobs connected with logging, such as hooking cabled logs to bulldozers—known as "choker setting"—so they could be hauled to the landing, working on the landing where the logs were stacked up for loading on trucks, and helping to load the trucks. But Harold had one other quality that made him gravitate to the type of woods job he finally selected. He was an independent-minded man, the kind of man who would have been a success as an old-time lumberjack as well as a modern worker in the woods. That's why he selected sawing. Sawyers generally do piecework—they are paid for the amount of timber they saw in a day. They can set their own hours as long as they produce the specified minimum amount. Harold liked this kind of challenge, invested in several models and sizes of power saws, and has been sawing ever since. He has worked in such states as Wyoming, Montana, Oregon, and California. He has sawed trees that range in size from the small lodgepole pines of Montana to the huge sugar pines of California. He has averaged at least $50 a day in his work, and on some jobs has made as much as $100 a day.

These days Harold Oliff confines his timber sawing activities to the winter months. The rest of the year he manages a wheat ranch in Montana. This combination is not unusual for woods workers. Many have their own small farms and ranches in the country where they find their employment.

Five Recent Graduates of a Technical School

All the following career examples happen to be graduates of the same school, Southeastern Illinois College, but many similar case histories could be obtained from the many other technical schools around the country.

Tom Arpasi of Poplar Bluff, Missouri, graduated from Southeastern Illinois in 1971. He went to work immediately for the Joseph G. Baldwin Company, a small blocking, box, and pallet company that has two mills, one in Poplar Bluff, Missouri, and the other in McLeansboro, Illinois. Today Joe is the owner-manager's right-hand man and will likely soon take over the entire operation. His main work is in wood procurement, and he has complete responsibility for mill inventory. He is also involved in the marketing of the company's products.

Rick Ebert of Tomahawk, Wisconsin, is a woodsman with Owens Illinois Corporation. "Woodsman" is their title for a forest technician. Rick graduated from technical college a year ago, but already he is making over $8,600 a year. His work involves all phases of timber management—cruising, marking trees for cutting, land surveying, and checking logging work.

Dan Senters of Manistee, Michigan, was twenty-six years old, married, and with two children when he decided to change careers and become a forestry technician. To do this, Dan left a job in a refinery in Joliet, Illinois, a job that was paying him $13,000 per year. But he wanted good outdoor work, and both he and his wife wanted to get out of the city. Dan was eligible for GI benefits and used these to finance his two years of forestry schooling. His wife, Beverly, worked at night, when Dan could look after the children. Dan had dropped out of high school, but gained a general equivalency degree while in the army. The college accepted him on that basis, and Dan graduated in June 1973 with honors, the first forestry student at Southeastern Illinois College to do so. Today he works for the Packaging Corporation of America, coordinating the efforts of pulpwood producers throughout the northern part of the lower peninsula of Michigan. No, he's not up to his oil refinery pay yet, though he soon will be, and may even surpass it in time. More importantly, Dan and family are living in country they like, and Dan is doing work he likes.

Bob Barnstable of Monroeville, Alabama, is a married veteran with one child. He is also an excellent student. When he graduated in May 1974, he received a number of good job offers. He accepted a position with MacMillan Bloedel Products, Inc. The company paid for his move to Alabama and put him and his family up in a motel until they could find suitable housing. He started with a salary of $8,400 a year as an assistant district ranger. His beginning work was cruising timber and writing management plans, and he will eventually be involved in all aspects of timber management, with regular promotions and salary increases.

Don Young of Dickson, Tennessee, also graduated from technical college in the spring of 1974. He secured employ-

ment with Moss American Company in general timber management and logging supervision throughout central Tennessee, excellent country for an outdoorsman like Don to work
in. He started with a salary of $8,770.

Donald E. Van Ormer, who helped train these men at Southeastern Illinois College, told me: "It is apparent that our best
placement has been with private industry. They are becoming
much more interested in the individual who is willing to spend
the majority of his career in the woods. Many professional foresters say they are willing upon graduation, but change their
tune after about a year and want to be V.P. of the company."

That gives you an idea then of what to expect if you attend
such a forestry college as Southeastern Illinois and apply yourself
diligently. You may not get to be vice president of the company
you end up working for (although you could), but you should be
able to make a decent living doing the kind of work you like, outdoors in good country.

FUTURE PROSPECTS

Because of inadequate budgets and manpower in recent
years the Forest Service has had to curtail operations. There are
millions of acres of national forestland that need timber stand
improvement, tree planting, and all the other services we must
supply if we are going to meet our timber product needs of the
future.

What is true on the national forests is just as true on other
federal timberlands and on state and private lands as well. The
greatest bloc of ownership of timberlands in the United States
is in the small holdings—farm woodlots, for example—where little
or no work has been done to improve productivity. If we are going to have a sufficient supply of wood products in the future, we
are going to need more Extension Service and Soil Conservation
Service work.

Here is what the Forest Service has to say about the future:

Employment opportunities for forestry aids [meaning also technicians] are expected to increase rapidly through the 1970's. Prospects will be especially good for those having post-high school training in a forestry curriculum. As the employment of foresters continues to grow, increasing numbers of forestry aids will be needed to assist them. Also, it is expected that forestry aids will assume some of the more routine jobs now being done by foresters.

For the present, if you are a newly graduated professional forester and haven't managed to find professional employment, take a slash piling or other menial labor job, if you have to, to get your start. Once you've made that start, you'll soon see your prospects improve.

Prepare yourself well, and you can have a fine future in the field of timber management.

For more information contact:

American Forest Institute
1619 Massachusetts Avenue N.W.
Washington, D.C. 20036

American Forestry Association
1319 18th Street N.W.
Washington, D.C. 20036

Society of American Foresters
1010 16 Street N.W.
Washington, D.C. 20036

Southern Forest Institute
Suite 280
One Corporate Square N.E.
Atlanta, Georgia 30329

Western Forestry and Conservation Association
1326 American Bank Building
Portland, Oregon 97205

2: YOUR CAREER IN SOIL SCIENCE AND CONSERVATION

Soil science is one of the oldest sciences known to man; yet at the same time it is one of the newest. Soil conservation began when agriculture did some 10,000 years ago. Classical authors wrote about it, and their writings prove that much knowledge about soil conservation had been accumulated by the time of the early Greeks and Romans. But as the explorations of Columbus and others enlarged the known world, men began exploiting the huge New World and forgot or ignored much of the wisdom of the ancients. It became common belief that the world was so vast that mankind would never lack for adequate land and resources to exploit, including new land for agriculture.

America was no exception. Rather, it became a classic example of land exploitation.

When the Europeans first came to these shores, North

America was the most lush and promising continent on earth. It was covered with forests and prairie grasses; it possessed a magnificent system of rivers and streams; it boasted the huge Great Lakes and other marvelous lakes and swamps. The Indians who lived in what is now the United States—an area of 1,903,000,000 acres—probably numbered less than 1 million. The Indians disturbed the land very little. They lived mostly from the products of the land—wild game, fish, and edible plants and nuts. Though they did practice some agriculture, and gave the European immigrants the secrets of raising such valuable food crops as corn, pumpkins, squash, and potatoes, their agriculture was quite limited and in no way hurt the land or other natural resources. The Indians were excellent conservationists, able to live with the bounty of the earth, and not exploit it badly.

The Europeans, once settled, practiced agriculture as their main means of livelihood. This was well and good, except that the rich, lush soil of America lulled them into a feeling of security. They thought such soil would never wear out. And even if one plot did wear out, so much land was available that they could easily move on to farm another place.

Too much land that would have been better left as forest was cleared for crops. Such cleared land produced well for a few years, but soon lost most of its fertility, and if it was steep land— as it often was—lack of the protective cover of trees and other vegetation allowed soil to wash away with each hard fall of rain.

The early settlers also mined the soil. Tobacco growing is one example. After the Indians taught the white man its use, tobacco became so important that it was often used as a medium of exchange. The thing to do was raise all the tobacco possible, year after year. That used up essential minerals in the soil.

Corn too became a chief crop, and it too wore out the soil if it was not rotated with other crops, such as legumes. But colonial farmers paid little heed to the consequences of the steady production of corn and tobacco. They cleared more and more of the forest to put more and more of the land into corn and tobacco. And when the land was sloping, erosion followed.

There were those who sought to warn against this despolia-
tion and tried to do differently. One was Thomas Jefferson, who,
like George Washington, had a great love for the land and for
agriculture. These two often exchanged information concerning
their common interest in agriculture. Both had large farms in
Virginia, where they spent as much time as they could, but from
which they often had to absent themselves to serve their country.

Jefferson adopted a program of soil conservation that was
unusual for his time. His system included crop rotations, with the
use of legumes and fertilizers, and deep plowing. He went on to
develop contour plowing on his steeper land, to keep that land
from eroding so readily. He was a pioneer in scientific agriculture in America, what we would call soil conservation today. But
most of his countrymen failed to heed his good example. They
continued to mine the land, subjecting it to bad erosion, and
when the land could no longer produce profitable crops, they
abandoned it for new land farther west and deeper south.

Up until nearly the time of the Civil War, the Carolinas and
Georgia were leading rice growing states, and the excellent rice
raised there commanded the highest prices on the world market.
But bad farming practices, and particularly the clearing of too
much of the forested highlands, subjected the lands to bad erosion and made it difficult to control the water resource so important for rice. After the Civil War these states were never again
principal rice growing regions. Instead much of the South
switched to cotton culture, and King Cotton became the basis of
the South's agricultural economy. But the problems of erosion
increased. Much of the best farmland had been lost or destroyed by the time this century began. And new land to exploit
was no longer so readily available. The land had suffered, and
the people began to suffer too.

WHAT IS SOIL CONSERVATION?

Hugh Hammond Bennett was born on his father's farm in
North Carolina in 1881. Many years later, after he had achieved

his reputation as America's foremost soil conservationist, he testified before a special subcommittee of the Committee on Agriculture, U.S. House of Representatives, and said this about conditions when he was a lad on his father's farm:

> All the individual activities taken together . . . were woefully inadequate to cope with the spreading land damage that was being caused by erosion. Farmers could see the damage . . . and they knew that yields were dropping off on many fields. They could see the gullies, they could see the abandoned fields and certainly they could see the abandoned farms that were showing up from place to place. But, as a general rule, all this was accepted by them, for some reason hard to explain, as something inevitable or a matter of course. . . .

Young Hugh Bennett, walking the eroded farmlands of North Carolina, decided he must do something about the terrible abuse of the land. He would dedicate his life to that. He would find out all he could about the science of soil conservation, then propagate the knowledge he had gained.

Bennett's career and Gifford Pinchot's were remarkably parallel, the one seeking to establish the science of soil conservation in America, the other the science of forestry, and both sciences were vitally needed to make the land and forests of America healthy and productive. They are two of the greatest men in the history of America, and they should be better known.

After he had gained his formal education, Dr. Hugh H. Bennett went to work for the U.S. Department of Agriculture's Bureau of Soils. He became an outstanding employee in that bureau, spending years examining and making soil surveys of land in various parts of the South. He began a crusade to stop bad farming practices and establish good soil conservation measures.

However, not until 1928 did the U.S. Department of Agriculture publish its first bulletin on soil conservation. The title was *Soil Erosion: A National Menace,* and the authors were H. H. Bennett and W. R. Chapline.

In America today there is disagreement on how to define soil conservation. Some consider it a separate subject. Others call it a combination of related sciences, including agriculture, forestry, soil science, biology, hydrology, economics, geology, environmental geography, and even ecology. For our purposes, we can turn to the organization that should know best, the Soil Conservation Society of America, for our definition of soil conservation: "A system of using and managing land based on the capabilities of the land itself, involving the application of the best measures or practices known, and designed to result in the greatest profitable production without damage to the land."

THE SOIL CONSERVATION SERVICE

Two things helped to focus the nation's attention on Bennett's crusade for soil conservation. One was the economic depression that struck in 1929 and lasted all through the 1930s. The other was Bennett's own persistence and dedication.

Things became so bad after the crash of 1929 that government leaders realized drastic measures would have to be taken to get the country back on course. In 1930, thanks to Bennett's persistence, Congress provided funds to the Department of Agriculture to conduct soil erosion investigations. Bennett was assigned to head up these studies. He did so with his customary thoroughness. And his findings were startling. He made known his estimation that enough soil was being washed out of American fields and pastures to load a train of freight cars that would encircle the earth eighteen times at the equator.

These studies, and the New Deal administration of President Franklin D. Roosevelt, led Congress in 1933 to establish a Soil Erosion Service in the Department of the Interior. Its responsibility was to apply knowledge of soil erosion and soil conservation on the farms of the country.

It was soon recognized, however, that the work of this new agency was allied more closely with the concerns of the agriculture than of the interior department, since it was primarily work needed on American farms. Therefore, in 1935 a long-time goal of Bennett's was realized: all soil erosion and soil conservation work was combined in a new agency, the Soil Conservation Service of the Department of Agriculture. Bennett was rightly named its first director.

With the support of Secretary of Agriculture Henry A. Wallace as well as President Roosevelt, Bennett soon got his new agency into high gear. One year after its founding, the SCS had 147 demonstration projects averaging 25,000 to 30,000 acres each, 48 soil conservation nurseries, 23 research stations, and 454 Civilian Conservation Corps camps under its jurisdiction. At the same time, more than 50,000 farmers had applied conservation plans on some 5 million acres of farmland.

Both Secretary Wallace and Dr. Bennett were firm believers in decentralized administration, for both were from rural backgrounds and shared the independent, democratic feelings most farmers have. They knew that for soil conservation to work best in America, the farmers themselves should be allowed to share in decision making. Again there is a remarkable parallel with the thinking of Gifford Pinchot, who pioneered such decentralized administration in setting up the Forest Service.

Agriculture Secretary Wallace, therefore, issued orders that beginning July 1, 1937, legally constituted soil conservation associations would thereafter coordinate all erosion control work on private lands. And in line with this thinking, in February 1937, President Roosevelt submitted to the governors of all the states a law authorizing farmers and ranchers to organize soil conservation districts in the various states. The legislatures of twenty-two states passed laws that same year which established this authority. The very first conservation district to be so established was in Anson County, North Carolina, Hugh Bennett's home county.

Thirty years later some 3,000 soil conservation districts had been established throughout the country, and they have been eminently successful in bringing the principles of good soil conservation directly to the farms and ranches of America.

WORKING FOR THE SCS

The SCS is today a large agency that constantly seeks qualified employees. It provides civil service protection and benefits.

Employees of the SCS work with people—all kinds of people —in the national program of soil and water conservation. Except for a staff of 300 in the Washington, D.C., office, the service's 15,000 employees are located throughout the fifty states, Puerto Rico, and the Virgin Islands. At the grass roots level, where the bulk of the conservation job is being done, the service works with landowners and land operators, local organizations and communities, and other agencies.

One of the service's primary responsibilities is to give technical help to soil conservation districts. But it has taken on wider tasks as the need for wiser use of resources has grown. These include a small watershed protection program, the Great Plains conservation program, the national cooperative soil survey, snow surveys and water forecasting, nonfarm conservation, resource conservation and development, and assistance in other agriculture department programs. I shall touch on some of these other SCS jobs in later chapters; here, emphasis is on soil science and conservation. Soil scientist, soil conservationist, and agronomist are the three main professions involved. Nonprofessional jobs as conservation aid or soil conservation technician are also available.

SOIL SCIENTIST

Soil scientists in the SCS are key men in the national soil, water, and resource conservation and development program. They provide soils information needed for land use planning on both agricultural and nonagricultural land. Their findings appear in published soil survey reports that are used by landowners and land operators, engineers, highway departments, planning and zoning bodies, builders, realtors, and others.

Soil scientists examine soils to identify the physical and chemical characteristics that affect the use and management of the land. They note differences in slope, erosion, geological formations, vegetation, and other features. They classify the soils into units that can be interpreted in terms of capability.

Further work involves collecting data on crop adaptability, yield, and response to different systems of management; grouping soils according to their capability; predicting yields of crops, grasses, and trees that can be produced under defined systems of management; forecasting physical behavior of soils in relation to engineering structures; and making interpretations for many other uses. Soil scientists also prepare guides that relate soil maps of an area to its recommended soil management practices.

In addition, soil scientists work in laboratories, where they analyze samples of soil, water, and vegetative materials to determine their physical and chemical properties.

The SCS provides intensive and specialized training under experienced leaders in all phases of soil science, both on the job and in group training centers.

New professional employees usually enter the SCS at grades GS-5 and GS-7. Higher grade positions normally are filled by promoting from within the service through the SCS career development and promotion plan.

To be a professional soil scientist, you will need a college degree with a major in soils or a related subject, such as agronomy, with at least fifteen semester hours in soils and other course work.

SOIL CONSERVATIONIST

Soil conservationists in the SCS work in rural and urban environments with all kinds of people in the national program of soil and water conservation. They bring to these people the

Soil scientists working near Redfield, South Dakota. Gene Webbis is taking a soil profile with a coring machine mounted on a pickup truck, while Donald Wilson records the soil log from the first core. (*U.S. Department of the Interior, Bureau of Reclamation*)

latest scientific and technical developments in soil and water conservation.

The work of the soil conservationist requires technical knowledge in such fields as agronomy, range management, forestry, wildlife biology, fishery biology, engineering, soils, and farm management. With this background he is able to analyze conservation problems and recommend a planned program for the land.

A soil conservationist may become experienced in all phases of soil and water conservation or may specialize in one field. He may be assigned to give technical help to a conservation district, usually the size of a county. He helps landowners and land operators prepare conservation plans. He gives technical advice on carrying out these plans.

The soil conservationist assists local sponsoring organizations in developing land treatment and structural measures for flood prevention, fish and wildlife development, recreation, and agricultural and municipal water supply in watersheds. He gives assistance in planning resource conservation and development projects, in solving land and water resource problems, and in improving the economic well-being of an area.

A soil conservationist needs a college degree with a major in soil conservation or a closely related agricultural science, such as agronomy or soils.

AGRONOMIST

Agronomists in the SCS conduct research on field crops involving varieties, breeding and selection, crop management, rotations, and weed control. Their work requires a good understanding of soil science and conservation.

Agronomists plan field experiments, execute the plans by planting and harvesting according to the experimental designs, make critical field observations by systematically recording notes, and complete the experiments by reporting results.

In the field of forage grasses, turf grasses, and legumes, they conduct research leading to the development of superior grasses and legumes, improved methods of establishment, and management practices that increase yield and quality.

Agronomists in the SCS provide technical guidance to landowners and land operators on agronomic phases of the soil and water conservation program and conduct field trials to evaluate adaptability and handling of grasses and legumes useful in soil and water conservation.

Basic requirements for a position as agronomist are a bachelor's degree from an accredited college or university with a major in agronomy or closely related subjects, including ten semester hours in crop production or plant breeding.

CONSERVATION AID

The conservation aid helps professional conservationists work up conservation farm plans. He helps farmers and ranchers establish measures called for in conservation plans. To qualify as a conservation aid in the SCS all you need is experience in conservation farming, with a farm or ranch background. The SCS hires many local residents with these qualifications to serve as conservation aids.

An aid can move up to a more technical job if he broadens his experience or takes the required courses at a technical school (see Appendix A). Though an aid's starting salary may be only $5,000 a year, most shortly make it to the five-figure annual pay bracket. Many aids run their own small farms in the areas where they are employed, and this supplements their incomes. And they have the satisfaction of knowing they are doing good and useful work in the outdoors.

SOIL CONSERVATION TECHNICIAN

The SCS hires soil conservation technicians, who start at the GS-4 grade but can advance quite a bit higher. You need take no written test to qualify as a GS-4 technician, but you must have successfully completed two academic years of study above the high school level in a junior or community college, technical institute, four-year college, or university. And your program of study must have included courses in such fields as engineering, agriculture, biology, physical science, drafting, or other subjects related to soil science and conservation. Lacking this, you need two years of technical experience on the job or in closely related jobs. A combination of two years of training and experience is also acceptable. One full academic year of study (generally thirty semester hours) is equivalent to one year of experience.

Morris Gardner, Soil Conservation Technician

Morris Gardner was employed for many years as a soil conservation technician for the SCS in Montana. During the summer he helped the soil conservationists advise farmers and ranchers on soil conservation matters and did much of the field work for the conservationists. During the winter he conducted snow measurements to be used in forecasting snow water runoff in the spring. He ran regular snow courses in the high mountain country, first on foot, later with a snow machine. It is an interesting, even fascinating job. And it is a vital job. By keeping monthly records of the snow courses and comparing them with the records of previous years, a good estimate of water runoff can be made. Floods can then be prepared for if necessary, and water available for irrigation can also be estimated.

Morris Gardner had another interest besides his regular employment with the SCS. He had his own small farm like so many employees of that agency, but in addition he was interested in auctioneering. He ran his own sales yard once each week, selling used merchandise for people, and this became one of the most popular activities in the county where he lives. After he retired he was able to devote even more activity to this interesting work. Recently he placed second in a statewide contest for auctioneers, a state where sales yards and auctioneering are common. His hobby-turned-profession enabled Morris to become acquainted with people all over his agricultural county, and this helped him in his work with the SCS.

EDUCATIONAL REQUIREMENTS AND OPPORTUNITIES FOR SCS WORK

Many colleges and universities offer qualifying courses in soil science and soil conservation. For example, the University of Wisconsin at Stevens Point offers the following subjects leading to a degree in soil science: soil profile description writing, techniques of soil and water conservation, forest soils, soil genesis and morphology, soil analysis, soils interpretation for land use planning, soil management, soil physics, soils field seminar, physical geography, landforms, air photo interpretation, physical geology, principles of range management, silvics, and agronomy.

As a student, you are eligible to become an employed student trainee in the SCS. Student trainee positions are available to college freshmen, sophomores, and juniors who are majoring in such subjects as soil conservation, agronomy, engineering, biology, soils, forestry, farm management, range management, animal husbandry, agricultural economics. Your work, done during your school vacations, prepares you to step into a full-time professional job with the SCS upon your graduation, at a better civil service grade than would otherwise be the case.

After you complete one year of college the SCS will hire you as a GS-3. Between your sophomore and junior years you will be eligible for GS-4, and between your junior and senior years you will be eligible for promotion to GS-5. When you graduate, you can, without additional civil service examination, be assigned a full-time professional job in the SCS, likely as a GS-7.

EMPLOYMENT OPPORTUNITIES OUTSIDE THE SCS

Besides the SCS, many other agencies hire qualified people for soil science and conservation work.

The Agricultural Research Service of the U.S. Department of Agriculture, as its name implies, is concerned with research work of all types dealing with agriculture. The service hires a wide variety of agricultural scientists, including soil scientists, who engage in a wide variety of agricultural research.

The Agricultural Stabilization and Conservation Service of the Department of Agriculture is mostly an administrative agency, and you'll see their branch offices in many farm communities throughout America. The ASCS administers such nationwide or regional programs as the rural environmental conservation program, the conservation reserve program of the soil bank, the cropland conversion program, cropland adjustment program (including public access and Greenspan, which is a program largely concerned with rural recreation and aesthetic improvement of the rural environment), Appalachian land stabilization and conservation program, and various commodity, annual set-aside, and price stabilization programs.

The Cooperative State Research Service of the Department of Agriculture administers federal grant funds for research in agriculture, forestry, resource conservation, and rural life made available to state agricultural experiment stations and forestry schools. This is largely a research agency, and it hires mostly well-educated agricultural scientists, who run the state agricultural experiment stations. The directors of these stations have a number of agricultural scientists on their staffs. They localize their research programs according to the needs of the individual state.

The Extension Service of the Department of Agriculture is a part of the Cooperative Extension Service. Administrative and technical personnel serve as liaison between agriculture department research and action agencies and the administrative and extension technical staffs at land-grant universities. County extension agents make available to farmers, homemakers, youth, and others the results of research conducted by the agriculture department, land-grant institutions, and other research agencies.

Extension is the agency you turn to for the latest information on what is going on in agriculture, either locally or nationally. It deals with such subjects as agriculture and natural resources, rural development, youth development (4-H and Future Farmers of America), international agricultural matters, and home economics. The agency is broken down into various divisions, and like most agricultural agencies, is decentralized in administration, with Extension Service leaders in the various states supervising the work of many local agricultural and forestry advisers. It employs mostly skilled professionals who have obtained master's, and in many cases doctor's, degrees.

The Forest Service of the Department of Agriculture is hiring an increasing number of soil scientists and conservationists. Many national forest supervisors have such scientists on their staffs now, and they are found in all regional offices of the Forest Service. Soil science technicians are also finding employment in this agency.

Military services—Air Force, Navy, and Army Corps of Engineers—hire soil scientists and technicians to help the millions of acres they control.

The Bureau of Indian Affairs of the Department of the Interior hires soil conservationists and technicians to help in managing the Indian reservations.

The Bureau of Land Management of the Department of the Interior hires many soil conservationists and technicians for help in managing the millions of acres of public lands it is responsible for.

The Fish and Wildlife Service of the Department of the Interior needs the services of soil scientists and conservationists in managing the national wildlife refuges.

The National Park Service, also of the interior department, has many soil scientists and conservationists on its payroll.

The Environmental Protection Agency needs soil scientists and conservationists to help it monitor federal land uses.

Merv Stevens, Soil Scientist in the Forest Service

Mervin E. Stevens is a soil scientist who elected to work in the Forest Service. While I have never discussed with Merv his reason for selecting the Forest Service, I suspect his having gone to school in Montana could be involved. That state of huge ranches and much irrigated valley agriculture also has many outstanding national forests. Merv is an avid outdoorsman and was particularly attracted to the woodlands for his outdoor recreation. Being also keenly interested in soils, he began to study edible wild plants and foods that grow in the forest and has become a recognized expert in this subject.

Merv has done well in the Forest Service. He rose rapidly in the organization and today, though still a relatively young man, holds the important position of assistant division chief for the Division of Lands, Minerals, Soils, and Watershed Management in the Eastern Region of the Forest Service. In this position he heads up all soil conservation work in the region, including soils management, soil management service, and soil surveys.

One of Merv's outstanding accomplishments has been the instigation of training of Chippewa Indians in Minnesota to become soil science technicians. The Indians received their formal training at Bemidji State College and their on-the-job training on the Chippewa National Forest. After they finished their training many were offered jobs as soil science technicians on the various national forests in the region.

Recently Merv Stevens returned from an assignment in Viet Nam, where he helped to make a study of the soils in that war-ravaged country and to train native students to become proficient in the science. This sort of opportunity comes to many government agency people, and the good work they do in countries around the world helps in building good will toward the United States. Few people are respected more than the United States scientists who come to give good advice and help a country achieve its potential. No job can be more important than teaching poor nations to raise more food for their people.

FUTURE PROSPECTS

Many parts of the world today are faced with famine. Food prices in the United States have never been higher than they are now, when much of our agricultural production goes to other countries. We no longer have the big reserves of grain we once had, and as a result, we are putting more and more of our land into agricultural production. As our own and the rest of the world's population continues to grow, our food needs spiral. The need for specialists in soil science and conservation is increasing.

The National Association of Conservation Districts has an

interesting pamphlet that emphasizes this need. It is called *A Resources Agenda for the 70's,* and in it are detailed the many jobs that must be done in soil conservation if we are to maintain the health and wealth of our land, without which we cannot grow the foodstuffs we shall need to survive.

This work will have to be done by the individual landowners, working in cooperation with the professionals, technicians, and aids in the SCS through local conservation districts. That means the scope of soil conservation work will have to increase greatly. For one thing, the national cooperative soil survey will have to be completed during the next decade. A national land use policy will have to be established. Comprehensive surveying and planning of the country's major river basins will have to progress, with participation by conservation districts and state soil and water conservation agencies, as a basis for the protection and orderly development of natural resources in relation to national needs.

As the career of Merv Stevens shows, soil scientists are in demand in many government agencies. And that demand will continue to grow because the public is well aware of the need to practice good environmental management. Care of the land, the soil, and other resources is basic. We can no longer tolerate the great amounts of soil erosion we have experienced in the past. Our future as a civilization depends on how we care for our land. Soil scientists and conservationists will play prominent roles in that drama of survival.

So important will they become that they are bound to find increasing career opportunities in the private sector. Heretofore, most graduates in soil science and conservation have had to turn to the government agencies for careers. But large scale agricultural enterprises are beginning to hire them now too, for these farms and ranches, if they are to continue in successful operation through the years, will have to give the same care to their land that the public is now demanding for public lands.

For more information contact:

National Association of Conservation Districts
1025 Vermont Avenue N.W.
Washington, D.C. 20005

Soil Conservation Society of America
1715 N.E. Ankeny Road
Ankeny, Iowa 50021

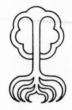

3: YOUR CAREER IN WATER CONSERVATION AND MANAGEMENT

Soil and water conservation are closely allied fields. Often they are combined.

Water has been called the most important natural resource of all. Man can exist for some time without food, but without water he will soon perish. Water does in fact sustain all life on earth.

But water can be a curse as well as a blessing. Year in and year out floods wreak more damage than any other type of natural disaster. And so coupled with water conservation must be the science of water management. The two are inseparable.

Water must be managed for another reason, besides that of controlling floods. There is more than enough water on earth to meet all man's needs now or in the foreseeable future. The problem is to get the water where it is needed.

Water conservation, like soil conservation, is one of the oldest sciences known to man. You can still find traces of ancient aqueducts and irrigation works in the oldest agricultural regions on earth. Very early man learned to guide the flow of water and to store it.

Ruins of ancient civilizations tell us another story. They tell us that when man mismanages his water resource he is doomed. The civilization known as Mesopotamia disappeared after flourishing a thousand years because heavy siltation clogged its many irrigation canals, and what were once highly productive agricultural lands became desert.

Overgrazing, which resulted in bad erosion and the subsequent siltation of the canals, caused Mesopotamia's undoing. The same thing happened in North Africa, once the breadbasket of the Roman Empire, but now the Sahara desert. And the story has been repeated in many other parts of the world. It could happen in America, too, in a much shorter time than in Mesopotamia and North Africa. That is why soil and water conservation is of the utmost importance, and why workers in both fields will be in continuing demand.

America was blessed with an abundance of water resources —great river systems, the inland seas known as the Great Lakes, and many other lakes and wetlands that we sometimes call swamps. We have done a poor job of conserving and managing this resource. Until this present century there was very little attempt at either. Even today we continue to neglect the water resource, despite the accumulating evidence that our neglect could bring down our civilization, and soon. Not only have we badly polluted some of our best water—we practically killed Lake Erie, for example—but we are still unable to manage water sufficiently to prevent disastrous floods. The toll of lives and property lost to floods continues to increase. Many cities have experienced water shortages, and these will grow worse if adequate steps are not taken to do a better job of water conservation.

That is the bad side of the coin. Fortunately, there is another side.

ESTABLISHMENT OF WATER CONSERVATION

In all fields of natural resource conservation there are always a few individuals who stand out among all others and become those voices crying out for change and warning of the consequences if change fails to come about. In forestry it was Gifford Pinchot. In soil conservation it was particularly Hugh Hammond Bennett.

In water conservation the man was George Perkins Marsh. He can truly be called the Father of Water Conservation in America, largely because of a book he published in 1864, entitled *Man and Nature.* In his book Marsh correctly stressed the need to look at an entire watershed in terms of stopping erosion and controlling floods. A well-forested watershed was the answer to good water conservation.

That is common knowledge today. But when Marsh published his book very little was known about this or any other aspects of water conservation. Though it was an old science, it had to be relearned and adapted to modern times. Marsh was aware of this and stressed the need for research and study so that more could be learned about water conservation. But Marsh was years ahead of his time, and America had to learn the hard way how right he was.

Some thoughtful people did read Marsh's book. It led them to take action.

In 1867 the Wisconsin State Legislature appointed a commission to study and report on the relation between forest cover and stream flow, one of the main things Marsh had advocated. And in the following year the state of New York established another commission to study water pollution, especially as it affected fish life. That led in 1872 to the appointment of the New York State Park Commission, composed of seven leading citizens who were charged with the investigation of forest conditions in the Adirondacks, the purpose being to benefit the Hudson River, the Erie Canal, and other waterways in the state. One of the results of that investigation was the establishment of the Adirondack Forest Preserve, the first such large preserve in any state.

The early forest preserves, or reserves as they were also called, were established mainly to protect the navigable waters and other streams in the United States. Massachusetts, as early as 1882, concerned with maintaining adequate municipal water supplies, authorized the acquisition of municipal forests for the protection of watersheds. In 1886 the American Forestry Congress went on record approving such action. And in 1891 the American Association for the Advancement of Science advocated adequate water conservation, particularly as it pertained to agriculture.

That same year—March 3, 1891—Congress passed the Forest Reserve Act, and this was followed on June 4, 1897, by the Organic Act for Forestry in America, which provided for the protection and administration of the forest reserves. An important clause in that act was that "no public reservation shall be established except to improve and protect the forest within the reservation or for the purpose of securing favorable conditions of water flows and to furnish a continuous supply of timber." Gifford Pinchot had a lot to do with the passage of that act. He knew that forestry and water conservation must go together.

With the turn of the century came renewed interest in water conservation, especially in the West which was now rapidly becoming settled. When Theodore Roosevelt became president, conservation gained a champion in the White House. While he was president two important new government agencies were established that had much to do with water conservation and management. One was the Forest Service, and the other was the Bureau of Reclamation.

THE BUREAU OF RECLAMATION

The Bureau of Reclamation is known today mostly for the large dams it has constructed in the West. But in its earlier days,

A water scientist taking a sample of water in the strip mine area of West Virginia.

when it went under the name of the Reclamation Service, it was known and respected for its other work in the field of water conservation. F. H. Newell was to this bureau what Pinchot was to forestry and Bennett was to soil conservation. Newell and Pinchot were contemporaries and also colleagues in fostering good conservation practices in the forests and along the waterways. Under Newell's leadership the Reclamation Service measured the western streams and, with the support of George H. Maxwell and the National Irrigation Congress, greatly advanced the irrigation of arid lands in the West.

Today the Bureau of Reclamation is charged with administering the federal program in western states for water resource development and use. The bureau's multipurpose projects involve fish and wildlife protection and recreational opportunities, water for farm irrigation and municipal and industrial use, hydroelectric power, and flood control.

WORKING FOR THE BUREAU OF RECLAMATION

ENGINEERS

The Bureau of Reclamation employs all types of engineers, but mainly its engineers deal with water conservation and management.

One of their jobs is to lay out canal systems and design their structures. They design earthfill and concrete dams, and even help decide the type of dam. Hydraulic engineers in the bureau design spillway systems for a river to improve flood control. They devise gates and valves to control safely and inexpensively the ever-increasing heads of water at the bureau's high dams. They develop improved and cheaper ways of lining canals to prevent loss of precious water. They even try to understand the weather better so that they can modify it where possible, to bend storms to their needs. They seek to control evaporation from desert reservoirs where every drop of water counts.

Hydrologists, who are also engineers, determine the characteristics of streams and the possibilities of floods, make snow surveys, and forecast runoff. They advise on water rights and the effect of a proposed project on the entire river basin.

The dams, power plants, reservoirs, water conveyance and distribution systems, and all the other facilities on reclamation projects must be properly operated and maintained to protect the more than $5 billion invested in these works. Many young engineers are employed to advise and guide the water users after they have taken over management of the bureau's irrigation facilities.

The young engineering graduate commencing a career with the bureau can eventually become fully qualified in any of the fields of work the bureau does, but only after a period of familiarization and training. The bureau's program for the young engineer introduces him to half a dozen or so different offices or sections as part of his orientation program.

A *Bureau of Reclamation Engineer*

A typical career pattern in the Bureau of Reclamation was followed by John Q. Doe (he wished to remain anonymous). Mr. Doe began his career with the bureau as a student trainee in 1948, and continued with the bureau following his graduation from the University of Denver in 1949 with a B.S. degree in chemical engineering. He became a materials engineer in the Applied Sciences Branch. He was responsible for many innovative uses of materials in bureau construction, maintenance, and repair programs. He was active in American Society of Testing and Materials (ASTM) projects related to reinforced thermosetting resin piping systems. He served on numerous in-house teams and committees, most notably as chairman of the bureau's Open and Closed Conduit Systems (OCCS) Committee and as a member of the California Undersea Aqueduct Study Management Team.

Today Mr. Doe heads up the Polymer Concrete and Structural Section in the Concrete and Structural Branch, Division of General Research, Engineering and Research Center, Bureau of Reclamation, Denver, Colorado. He is responsible for the research and development of concrete polymer materials for bureau application and for the structural research and testing of unique structures for bureau projects.

During his career, Doe has worked on almost all major projects and structures built by the bureau and has authored numerous technical articles and reports published in a variety of media. As an engineer with the Bureau of Reclamation he finds his work challenging and never dull.

AIDS AND TECHNICIANS

Technical aids are hired by the Bureau of Reclamation at the grades of GS-2 and GS-3. Most of the technical aid jobs are in

A plant physiologist of the Agricultural Research Service and a chemist of the Bureau of Reclamation examine aquatic weeds grown for test purposes. (*U.S. Department of the Interior, Bureau of Reclamation*)

rural areas helping engineers and surveyors who work on dams and other water conservation projects. To qualify as a GS-2, you need six months of actual work experience similar to that for which you would be hired, and that can cover quite a wide range —construction work, farm work, and the like. To qualify as a GS-3 you need one year of this kind of work experience.

Technician jobs in the bureau range from GS-4 to GS-12, meaning annual salaries of from $7,198 to $17,397, based on 1974 wage rates. Since the GS-12 technician can eventually earn more than $20,000 a year, the bureau is an attractive agency to work for.

In lower grade positions, employees typically work as aids to professional engineers, scientists, or higher grade technicians. At the higher grades assignments may be comparable in difficulty to those of professional engineering positions. Positions in this occupation do not require training equivalent in type and scope to a professional engineering curriculum. Many of the technical schools listed in Appendix A will qualify you.

EMPLOYMENT OPPORTUNITIES
OUTSIDE THE BUREAU

ARMY CORPS OF ENGINEERS

The Army Corps of Engineers is one of the oldest agencies in the government. It dates back to Revolutionary times. Not only did it help in the fight for independence; after the Revolution, when our infant nation needed many internal improvements, our leaders turned to skilled army engineers for the technical know-how. These engineers founded the first engineering school and built lighthouses, harbors, bridges, and railways. They opened river highways for the settlers of the interior, explored the deserts and mountains of the West, and began improving our canals, waterways, and harbors. Their mission grew further to encompass many forms of conservation and development work affecting water and related land resources—flood control, public water supply, power, recreation, fish and wildlife conservation.

You don't have to join the army to work for its Corps of Engineers. It has approximately 45,000 civilian employees. They work in every state of the union and in more than ten nations overseas. The types of programs in which they engage are extraordinarily diverse.

In water resources planning and management, the Corps of Engineers looks to hydrologists. The working relations at corps installations are, however, interactive and dynamic. For example, if you enter as a hydrologist you will have many opportunities to rise above a narrow specialty or sphere of interest. The Army Corps of Engineers is the largest engineering organization in the free world and has a profound new commitment to preserving and enhancing our natural environment.

The Institute for Water Resources is the organization within the corps that is responding to the changing needs of America by developing improvements in water resources. The institute conducts research in environmental and social values as well as economic values. In marked contrast to former days, economic efficiency is no longer considered the primary goal.

The burgeoning importance of planning has opened up great new career opportunities. At the same time it has required new training and education designed to prepare future corps planners to deal with changing concepts of water resources management and gain a firm understanding of the options and alternatives available.

Current corps programs embrace constant study of every major river basin and many other water areas. Operating responsibilities of the corps include over 22,000 miles of waterways, one of the most extensive navigation systems in the world. The corps' regulatory responsibilities include the issuance of permits for work in the waterways to ensure that such work is consistent with the public interest. The corps issues discharge permits, under the Refuse Act permit program, to control what is discharged into our waterways.

The corps has placed in operation about 700 projects that provide flood control and related benefits. Maintaining these requires much skilled help.

The corps' water resources development program has involved work for all purposes costing some $20 billion, and new appropriations are in excess of $1 billion a year.

In addition to all the above, it is the Corps of Engineers that is called upon in times of natural disaster for rescue and rehabilitation of affected areas.

THE TENNESSEE VALLEY AUTHORITY

The TVA, primarily a water management agency, hires many professionals and technicians to administer and direct this important activity.

It has built or acquired twenty-eight major dams. Nine are on the Tennessee River, eighteen are on tributary streams, and one is in the Cumberland Valley. Two more major tributary dams are under construction at this time. Six other major dams in the Tennessee River system, owned by the Aluminum Company of America, have been integrated with the operation of TVA dams for mutual benefit.

Water quality management activities, which date from the TVA's early role in encouraging the valley states to establish effective pollution control programs, were intensified in the 1960s. Working with state and local agencies, the TVA helps to assure effective treatment of waste from commercial and industrial developments along the lakeshores and from floating craft on the lakes. It conducts extensive water quality monitoring and research.

Water and the way it is used are as vital to the Tennessee Valley today as in 1933, but the purposes water must serve today are more varied and require more complex planning. To learn more about the effects of increased water temperature on aquatic life, the TVA and the Environmental Protection Agency (EPA) have planned a large experimental facility at the Browns Ferry Nuclear Plant. The TVA is also engaged in experiments to determine beneficial uses of heated water from power plants —for greenhouse and field production of high-value crops, commercial fish production, and heating and cooling for livestock and poultry housing.

Another area of TVA study is the possible effects on water quality of plant nutrients washed off by rain or dissolved into groundwater from land where agricultural fertilizers have been applied. These studies include analysis of conditions in small, controlled watersheds that allow researchers to account for all water that enters and leaves and all fertilizer that is applied, and to assess the relation between the two. The subject is a complex one because soil characteristics, rainfall and other hydrological conditions, and fertilizer use vary from one area to another.

THE GEOLOGICAL SURVEY

The Geological Survey of the U.S. Department of the Interior conducts water studies to establish firm foundations for planning and monitoring maximum development and safe use of the nation's water resources. Some 1,600 research and basic data projects are under way, including the measurement of quantity and quality of water at about 50,000 sites—streams, estuaries, lakes, reservoirs, wells, and springs. Most of the projects are carried on in cooperation with state, local, and federal agencies. Special purpose studies include delineation of location and frequency of flooding in metropolitan areas as a guide to floodplain occupancy and zoning; analysis of causes, effects, and possible solutions of other urban hydrological problems; and regional and river basin appraisals of hydrological systems in sufficient detail to explain and predict the flow and quality characteristics

Hydrologists on the Potomac River moving a hoist into position. (*U.S. Department of the Interior, Geological Survey*)

of rivers, the interrelated influences of groundwater, and the effects of human activities upon the systems.

For water-related jobs with the Geological Survey write:

Chief Hydrologist
Mail Stop 409
Geological Survey National Center
Reston, Virginia 22092

THE SOIL CONSERVATION SERVICE

The SCS is concerned with water conservation problems because these relate directly to soil and its use or misuse.

Irrigation in the United States until relatively recent times was largely confined to lands that required the application of twelve inches or more of supplemental waters, commonly called the full irrigation supply. These semiarid lands mostly were

A hydrologist measuring stream flow at Rock Creek Park. (*U.S. Department of the Interior, Geological Survey*)

A water milfoil spraying operation on a lake.

west of the 100th meridian (which runs from the Dakotas down through Texas) and received less than twenty inches of precipitation a year. In modern times much irrigation is being done east of the 100th meridian, in the semihumid zones of the Middle West, and throughout the prairie states. Each year sees more irrigation being carried on in humid zones where farmers generally have never before seriously contemplated its use. Irrigation assures not only more stable crop production, but also more intensive production with higher yields. Our increasing food needs have made this essential.

One of the most uncertain factors of farm production is the supply of water. If the farmer is accurate in his forecast of the extra water supply he needs, he is a successful producer; but if he estimates his irrigation needs wrongly, he fails. The variation in rainfall during the annual growing season makes it hard to determine irrigation needs. Knowing how much irrigation water will be available during the growing season is also vital. That's why the SCS and other agencies maintain snow measurement courses during the winter, in which not only the snow depth but the water content of the snow are measured. That's why, too, SCS technicians and professionals advise farmers on the best application of water to their land, making every drop yield maximum results.

The SCS and other agencies must work on many problems connected with the establishment and expansion of irrigation on a permanently sound basis. One problem concerns the acidity or alkalinity of soil, either of which affects the availability for plant growth of nutritional elements in a soil. Soils in arid climates often develop heavy concentrations of harmful salts. In the West, therefore, new lands being irrigated for the first time are tested to ensure that conditions are favorable for plant growth. Excessively acid or alkaline soil can often be improved by applying soil amendments such as gypsum or by leaching out the harmful concentrations.

Another problem is how to dispose of unused irrrigation waters. And associated with the problem of controlling excess water is the need to conserve the resource. All this adds up to many jobs with the SCS in the field of water conservation and management.

THE BUREAU OF LAND MANAGEMENT

The Bureau of Land Management hires both professionals and technicians to do watershed management work on the hundreds of millions of acres of land it manages in the western states. The watershed management program provides an excellent career opportunity in the bureau. The work includes the installation and maintenance of land treatment and water control structures necessary to conserve the soil resource and to improve watershed conditions. It provides for soil stabilization (as influenced by both wind and water erosion), improves water quality, and reduces off-site and on-site damage from flooding and soil erosion.

The watershed management program is directed primarily at 123 million acres in the western states that are considered to

be in a deteriorating or only fair condition. Intensive land treatment is required on 45 million acres of this total, which are
classed as frail lands. Treatments may include water spreading,
brush control, seeding, contour furrowing and pitting, and deep
tillage. In addition, other acreages receive direct watershed
treatment in the form of check and detention dams, diversions
and drop structures, water development, and related land treatment practices.

THE FOREST SERVICE

The U.S. Forest Service is very much in the water conservation and management business. Forestlands, totaling one third
of the land area of the continental United States, yield over 60
percent of the annual stream flow in the forty-eight contiguous
states.

In the eleven western states, more than half the stream flow
comes from the national forests, which occupy 21 percent of the
area. In the East, national forestlands are located largely in the
watershed uplands and yield large quantities of high quality
water.

That's why there are water conservation specialists on every
forest supervisor's and every regional forester's staff. In addition,
the numerous forest and range experiment stations conduct much
water conservation research on the national forests. The researchers often establish projects that demonstrate their findings.

THE FISH AND WILDLIFE SERVICE

The Fish and Wildlife Service has the responsibility under
the Fish and Wildlife Coordination Act to (1) investigate and
report on water resource development projects prior to their
construction or license by the federal government, (2) determine
the probable effects of such projects on fish and wildlife resources and associated habitats, and (3) recommend measures
for preventing or reducing damage to and improving conditions

for these resources. The bureau also advises and consults on environmental impacts of proposed federal and federally assisted or licensed actions in connection with Section 102 of the National Environmental Policy Act, on the establishment of water quality standards and criteria, and on the operations criteria of certain federal reservoirs and systems. The bureau diverts and impounds water in connection with its national wildlife refuge and fish cultural programs.

The Missouri River Basin studies staff of the bureau prepares and reviews reports of water development projects sponsored by other federal agencies in the Missouri Basin.

OTHER AGENCIES

Still other agencies, state as well as federal, hire hydrologists and other water conservation and management specialists. Many states have state water boards or the equivalent, which are charged with managing the state's water resources. They often employ hydrologists, irrigation specialists, riparian rights experts, and the like. In addition, hydrologists and other water specialists work in the Extension Service and at the state agricultural colleges and experiment stations.

FUTURE PROSPECTS

Hydrologists and other water specialists are in demand now, and they are going to be in even greater demand in the future. A few examples will show why.

The work of the Bureau of Reclamation continues to grow simply because the West itself continues to grow. What is called the Reclamation West is the fastest growing part of the country. There were 27 million people living in the seventeen westernmost reclamation states in 1940. These states have since grown at a rate that is twice the national rate, and by the end of the century it is believed that as many as 100 million people may be living in this big part of the country. A tremendous amount of skilled water conservation and management will be required to meet the needs of so many people.

The SCS will also have much to do in water conservation and management in the future. It has been estimated that only some 43 percent of upstream areas have been given adequate land treatment to conserve and better control water movement. Agricultural damage is estimated roughly at about two thirds of all upstream damage. If we are to meet the food needs of the future, this damage must be stopped.

Those are just two examples; many more could be given. The future looks bright for those interested in a career in water conservation. The pay is good now, as good as for comparable scientific jobs in other agencies, and it will continue to compare favorably.

For further information contact:

American Water Resources Association
206 East University Avenue
Urbana, Illinois 61801

National Water Resources Association
897 National Press Building
Washington, D.C. 20004

National Watershed Congress
Room 1105
1025 Vermont Avenue
Washington, D.C. 20005

National Waterways Conference, Inc.
1130 17th Street N.W.
Washington, D.C. 20036

Water Resources Council
Suite 800
2120 L Street N.W.
Washington, D.C. 20037

4: YOUR CAREER IN WILDLIFE AND FISHERIES MANAGEMENT

According to scientific estimates, there were once 60 million buffalo, 1 million moose, 10 million elk, 2 million wolves, 400 million beaver, 40 million antelope, and billions of passenger pigeons in America. There are many fewer of these animals now, and some, like the passenger pigeon, are gone forever.

Does it make any difference? Is wildlife all that important? It is indeed, because man's own survival depends upon the kind of healthy environment necessary for wildlife survival. There are also economic and aesthetic reasons for maintaining healthful numbers of wildlife. Billions of dollars are spent each year for sport hunting and fishing. Millions of people engage in these sports, while millions more enjoy observing wildlife in its native habitat—in the national parks, on the national forests and national

wildlife refuges. These millions agree there is still another fundamental reason for preserving wildlife—the moral reason. Wildlife
does have the right to inhabit our planet Earth, along with the
rest of us. Because so many of man's activities are detrimental to
wildlife, it is his duty to engage in other activities that will at
least assure sufficient numbers of wildlife for species survival.

WHAT IS WILDLIFE MANAGEMENT?

Wildlife management is a good and useful science. It is also
a relatively new science. Until about forty years ago, when Aldo
Leopold published his studies, those who worked with fish and
wildlife resources were more protectors than scientific managers
and investigators. Protection is still important, but wildlife management today is a complex, diversified field, with room for many
different kinds of specialists.

Aldo Leopold, who began his career with the Forest Service,
has good claim to the title Father of Wildlife Management. The
publication of his book, *Game Management,* in 1933 marked the
true beginning of wildlife management as a science in America.
He later became head of the Wisconsin Department of Conservation and made it one of the best in the nation, a reputation it still
enjoys, though it is now combined with other state agencies in
the Department of Natural Resources. A similar combination of
agencies has taken place in many other states.

Research has become increasingly important in wildlife
management science. Research centers, known as cooperative
wildlife research units, have been established at many colleges
around the country, and they employ many wildlife management
scientists as well as graduate students in investigating wildlife
problems in the field.

One of the revolutionary concepts Leopold established is
that the health of wildlife depends primarily on habitat. He
taught the uselessness of providing big game refuges and stocking them with wildlife, but failing to improve the habitat. Good

habitat is the important thing. The animals will stock the healthy habitat themselves. He also pointed out the need for predators to control the wildlife population and maintain the balance between the habitat and the wildlife it supports—a balance essential to the continuing health of both.

Thanks to Leopold and other wildlife leaders, important legislation was passed by Congress. The laws have brought about better wildlife management and created many useful jobs at the same time.

The first such law was the Migratory Bird (Duck) Hunting Stamp Act of 1934. The second was the Federal Aid in Wildlife Restoration Act of 1937, commonly known as the Pittman-Robertson (P-R) Act.

The Duck Stamp Act created a fund for the purchase of wetlands, thus creating the better habitat Leopold advocated. It also enabled better enforcement of hunting laws, making it a federal rather than just a state offense to illegally kill federally protected waterfowl and other migratory birds.

Nothing better has happened for wildlife than the P-R Act. The funds it controls are derived from an 11 percent federal excise tax on guns and ammunition. These funds are allocated to the states on a matching basis of 75 percent federal funds and 25 percent state funds. The act has enabled the states to underwrite programs they could not otherwise have undertaken, and to hire thousands of wildlife management scientists to activate these programs. P-R funds are used to restore and improve living conditions (habitat) for game birds and animals. Federal aid projects have included research, land acquisition, construction and development of wildlife areas, and the maintenance of completed work.

An example of outstanding P-R work is that done by the Fish and Game Division of the Indiana Department of Natural Resources in wild turkey restoration. In the southern part of the state, in cooperation with the Hoosier National Forest, Gerald Wise and other biologists in the Fish and Game Division studied and utilized the specially created Mogen Ridge Turkey Management Area on the national forest to bring back the wild turkey in goodly numbers. Today, thanks to their work, you can once again hunt this magnificent wild bird in Indiana and enjoy seeing it in its native habitat. Biologists like Wise may still not be as well paid as they should be, but the fringe benefits of doing work they love in country they love are substantial.

Deer management has been a spectacular success in the field of wildlife management. Elk management has also been notable. Various species of grouse have made a good comeback. The black bear has returned to many places where it was once common. The antelope is again seen on the prairies. But the grizzly bear is having a more difficult time, as is the wolf. The trumpeter swan seems to have been saved from extinction, but the fate of the whooping crane is still precarious. And so it goes. The work of the wildlife management scientist is still vital.

WHAT IS FISHERIES MANAGEMENT?

America in its early days was as blessed with fish as with other forms of wildlife. Protective laws dealing with fisheries go back even further than laws dealing with game animals.

Fishing as a sport has long been more popular than hunting in America, and protective laws were considered necessary to maintain an adequate supply of fish. Fishing licenses were the result, and they provided funds for fisheries work. Thus, the American sportsman has contributed the principal means for financing essential programs in the protection and restoration of fish and game resources. Some people today decry hunting, and even fishing, as cruel sports. But done properly, as laws dictate they must be done, fishing and hunting are good and even necessary to keep fish and game numbers in healthy balance.

Habitat is as important in fisheries as it is in game management. Without good habitat in the streams and lakes you cannot have a good fishery resource.

The Dingell-Johnson (D-J) Act of 1950 did for fisheries science what the earlier Pittman-Robertson Act did for game management. It authorized a federal aid program of fish restoration and, by providing matching funds, gave the states the means to engage in fish conservation work.

The D-J program has not only saved fishing in many places, but has brought about many new opportunities for enjoying the sport throughout America. It has enabled all state fish and game departments to add fisheries scientists to their staffs, and this has brought about a dynamic program of fisheries research coupled with much improved fish habitat. The D-J program has also made it possible for the states to provide better public access to fishing waters, has improved hatchery and stocking methodology, and through its research has jettisoned outmoded laws and brought about better fisheries regulation and management concepts.

This work is just getting a good start. Much more research is needed to determine what constitutes the best fisheries management. The scientists will be best equipped to supply that answer, for in becoming fishery experts they must study such complicated yet relevant subjects as water pollution, limnology (the study of the life and phenomena of lakes, ponds, and streams), oceanography (since many fish are salt water inhabitants), ichthyology (the study of fish themselves), fish culture, fishery management, nutrition of fish, fishery biology, and parasitology as it involves fish diseases.

THE PUBLIC LANDS

According to the Public Land Law Review Commission, there are 26.6 million acres of land under the jurisdiction of the Fish and Wildlife Service of the U.S. Department of the Interior. Over 17 million acres of these lands are set aside and administered primarily for resident game species. Most of the other 9 million acres constitutes migratory bird refuges.

Many more millions of acres on the other public lands—those administered by the Forest Service and the Bureau of Land Management—are places where many forms of wildlife find good habitat. Almost all of Alaska's 365 million acres are wildlife habitat of one kind or another, and 348 million acres of this huge state are still in federal ownership. Some of the largest caribou and moose herds in North America use the public lands in Alaska. The marshes and muskeg and river deltas of our northern state are the summer nesting areas for millions of North America's migratory waterfowl. The streams and rivers that flow to the sea are the spawning runs for much of the North Pacific salmon fishery.

In the continental forty-eight states, public land constitutes 6 percent or more of the total land in twenty of those states. Of the federal land in those twenty states, 315 million acres are classed as big game habitat. These lands provide the principal habitat for between 40 and 48 percent of the big game populations in those states. Nearly all the elk, bighorn sheep, mountain goat, moose, and wild turkey in these states are primarily dependent on the public lands for their survival. At the same time, the lakes, streams, and rivers on federal lands account for 45 percent of the cold and warm water fish habitat on the West Coast, 71 percent in the mountain states, and 15 percent in the eastern states.

The states have traditionally regulated the taking and transport of fish and wildlife within their borders, whether that wildlife was taken on state, private, or federal lands. Historically the states have regulated the game population of federal lands, and the federal government has managed the habitat. However, since effective wildlife population management involves habitat management as well, the states are becoming increasingly concerned with programs of habitat management and with the effect of other public land activities on wildlife habitat.

Similarly the federal land managing agencies have developed policies and programs of their own on the lands they administer. Much of the habitat work they do on public land is the same kind of work the states do or would like to do, and much of it is done cooperatively with the states.

Other forms of recreation involving wildlife, such as bird watching and photography, have greatly increased in popularity and are being given more consideration by public land managers. Under new guidelines nongame species are given equal treatment with game species in public land management.

The federal government formally assumed a national responsibility for protecting rare or endangered species of native fish and wildlife in the Endangered Species Act of 1966. Some areas of public lands have already been set aside to protect disappearing species, such as the California condor and the Kirtland warbler, which nests only on the Manistee National Forest in Michigan. There will be more of these set-asides and more need to study these rare and endangered species to determine the best way to preserve them.

By statute, the national parks and monuments are in most cases closed to public hunting. One of the major purposes of park administration is to protect and preserve the wildlife and fish for public enjoyment and appreciation. The Public Land Law Review Commission has recommended that the statute prohibiting hunting in the parks and monuments be continued. But at the same time the commission suggested that special measures might be necessary to control the numbers of big game in parklands—in Yellowstone, for example, where excessive numbers of elk have seriously depleted the habitat. Controlled shooting has taken place in some parklands. More often the federal government and the concerned states work cooperatively to harvest the excess game animals as they migrate out of the parks. This calls for work by game managers, both on the federal and state level. A game manager must have a degree in wildlife management or associated biological sciences.

EMPLOYMENT OPPORTUNITIES

THE FISH AND WILDLIFE SERVICE

This organization has a primary federal responsibility to help conserve and manage the nation's fish and wildlife resources. Its program provides public opportunities for understanding, appreciating, and using these endowments.

The service applies information from laboratory and field studies to develop, manage, and maintain a national system of fish hatcheries for propagating sport fish and a national system of wildlife refuges for conserving wildlife. Particular attention is given to managing migratory game birds and protecting and preserving endangered native species.

Professional Jobs

This means the employment of fishery and wildlife biologists, as well as refuge managers, who are usually also wildlife biol-

Collecting fish spawn. (*Wisconsin Natural Resources Department*)

ogists. The pay scale ranges from GS-5 to GS-15. If you are planning a professional career in fish or wildlife biology, you may wish to inquire about student trainee programs, which are sometimes in operation in the service's regional offices.

Nonprofessional Jobs

The service also employs nonprofessional workers—maintenance men, laborers, and skilled tradesmen such as carpenters, masons, electricians, and the like. A few such positions exist at most of the national wildlife refuges and national fish hatcheries and are covered by appropriate U.S. Civil Service Commission examinations.

Fishery aids and wildlife aids are employed in small numbers at the national fish hatcheries and national wildlife refuges. The pay scale ranges from GS-2 through GS-5. These aids assist the professional biologists who manage the field programs.

Inquiries regarding the appropriate civil service examination for nonprofessional positions should be directed to the near-

Chemical rehabilitation by fisheries workers. (*Wisconsin Natural Resources Department*)

est U.S. Civil Service Commission regional office or interagency board.

Most summer jobs in the service are in grades GS-1 through GS-4 and are filled from registers of names supplied by the U.S. Civil Service Commission of successful candidates in the Civil Service Commission summer examination. Literature about this examination is updated annually by the commission and may be obtained from the commission office nearest you.

STATE AGENCIES: WISCONSIN

The individual states are by far the largest employers of fish and game workers, including research workers, managers, and conservation officers (also called game wardens).

An example is Wisconsin, long a bellwether state for fish and game management, thanks to such men as Aldo Leopold and Ernest Swift. In recent years Wisconsin has regrouped its various conservation agencies into one master department of natural resources. Fish and game administration is now part of this all-encompassing department, which includes such other types of administration as parks management and forestry. Many other states—for example, Illinois, which has developed one of the best departments in the Middle West—have done the same.

Professional Jobs

The beginning fish and game worker in Wisconsin is hired as a natural resources specialist 1. Under this heading come such specific jobs as fish manager or biologist, game biologist, and game manager.

The fish manager or biologist performs professional and scientific work in relation to the propagation, distribution, protection, and management of fish or other aquatic resources. He may act as a project leader on a minor research project or a project assistant on a major project. He may carry on general fish management work in an assigned area. He participates in established courses of instruction. He may also assist in forest fire control or act as a conservation warden.

Required training and experience for fish manager or biologist consist of graduation from a college or university with major courses in the biological sciences with emphasis on fishery biology or fish management. Candidates with a master's degree may be given preference for research positions.

The game biologist performs professional and scientific work in relation to wildlife management, acts as project assistant on a major wildlife research project, and participates in established courses of instruction. He too may assist in forest fire control or conservation warden duty.

Required training and experience include graduation from a college or university with major courses in the biological sciences with emphasis on wildlife management or wildlife biology. Candidates with a master's degree may be given preference for research positions.

The game manager carries on general game management work in an assigned area, assists in cooperative work assignments with other department bureaus, assists in public relations and educational programs related to natural resources, and performs related work as required.

Needed training and experience include graduation from a college or university with (1) a major in wildlife management or wildlife biology, (2) a major in agronomy, a biological science, forestry, or soils with emphasis on wildlife biology or wildlife management, or (3) an equivalent combination of training and experience.

You do not have to be a resident of Wisconsin to qualify for any of these three positions. To apply, write:

Wisconsin State Bureau of Personnel
1 West Wilson Street
Madison, Wisconsin 53702

Department of Natural Resources
Box 450
Madison, Wisconsin 53701

Or you can stop at any state office and request a Wisconsin career candidate brochure and application.

Nonprofessional Jobs

Other jobs in the Wisconsin Department of Natural Resources have less demanding educational requirements. However, Wisconsin residency is required for park ranger 1, forest conservation technician 1, conservation aid, and other nonprofessional positions. Some experience in outdoor work and an aptitude for that work are also necessary. A year or two in one of the technical schools listed in Appendix A would enhance your employability.

Eligibility requirements are becoming stricter for the job of conservation warden (game warden) as its scope broadens to include much information and education work. A college degree in wildlife management or other biological science is becoming more common, and salaries are also improving.

Wisconsin's beginning salary for all conservation warden and natural resources specialist positions is $695 a month, with the first salary increase of $30 coming after six months, and promotion to grade 2 after approximately one year of on-the-job training. Systematic merit increases take the job holder up to a maximum of $974 a month. That's about par in most states.

The value of the technician is becoming better appreciated in state fish and game work. Some of the two-year vocational schools offer courses that give this training. In Wisconsin, for example, Nicolet College at Rhinelander, and Oshkosh Technical Institute in Oshkosh offer training in woods work, conservation technician work, wildlife management, and related areas.

It's a good idea to go to school in the state where you wish to work—not only to establish your residency, but also to acquaint yourself with the fish and game management situation in that state. It's only natural for state employment officers to look with favor upon those applicants who reside in the state, everything else being equal.

STATE AGENCIES: MONTANA

Montana is where some of the most exciting fish and game work in the country is being done today. That state is still blessed with blue-ribbon trout streams and has some of the finest big game hunting to be found anywhere. It has a progressive department of fish and game that works under the commission system, with commission members appointed by the governor. One of the members of the Montana Fish and Game Commission is Dr. W. Leslie Pengelly. He is known nationally as a fish and wildlife authority and is a professor in the school of forestry at the University of Montana in Missoula.

Because Montana is such a popular state to live and work in, the competition for fish and game positions is fierce. For example, only 6 to 8 game wardens are hired every two years, but as many as 300 apply for these jobs.

Professional Jobs

Vern Craig, veteran of the Montana Fish and Game department, informs me that the field of fish and game biology is saturated with personnel. But he goes on to say: "This situation should improve, however, and could possibly improve greatly."

With the exception of hatchery personnel, most fisheries positions in Montana are related to biology and require an academic background. Craig reports "little turnover in hatchery personnel, and no indications the program will be greatly expanded." As a matter of fact, Montana has reduced its hatchery program in recent years, giving greater emphasis to improving habitat conditions for wild fish. However, hatchery-bred fish will continue to be important in the more populous parts of the country because fishing pressure is too great for the native wild species to withstand.

As in fisheries, most of the game division positions require a degree in biology, according to Craig. There is a limited number of managerial positions on game ranges, and in recent years Montana has been acquiring more of these ranges, particularly for winter feeding of game, always a crucial factor in the high mountain country common in Montana. Do not confuse these with game preserves. The game preserves, where hunting is not allowed, will become things of the past if game biologists have their way. Game preserves have proved inadequate for sustaining game populations. On most game ranges hunting is allowed in season.

Practical experience and scientific knowledge are the requirements for game range manager in a state like Montana. A college degree is mandatory; the practical experience must usually be acquired on the job.

Claude Smith, Range Manager

Claude Smith is manager of the important Bitterroot Game Range in Montana. Divided into two large segments, this 9,000-acre range lies in the upper foothills of the Sapphire Mountains along the east side of the large Bitterroot Valley. I knew Claude when he was a rancher in the Bitterroot's Burnt Fork country. He is an exception among game range managers in states like Montana, but an exception that proves the rule. Practical experience as a rancher and many years as a hunter and observer of big game taught Claude what he needed to be a successful range manager. He knows how to care for grasslands, and he knows about big game biology and habits. He also has good practical knowledge—how to build the best types of fences, cattle guards, and roads on the range. Thus, though he lacks the college degree that is now a standard requirement for game range managers, Claude Smith, in the eleven years he has managed the Bitterroot Game Range, has brought its badly overgrazed lands back to healthy, lush grasslands that today provide excellent habitat for large herds of elk and deer.

Nonprofessional Jobs

Game wardens in Montana protect, preserve, and propagate game and fur-bearing animals, fish, and game birds; investigate violations of state and federal statutes; apprehend and arrest violators; gather and present evidence; represent the Department of Fish and Game at local meetings of civil and sportsman groups; gather information about game and fish populations and distribution; investigate complaints about nuisance game animals; and see that all those who hunt, fish, or take game, fur-bearing animals, game birds, or fish have the necessary licenses.

To be an effective game warden or conservation officer for a state fish and game department like Montana's takes a good deal of self-reliance and good physical condition. The warden generally works alone, sometimes under difficult and ticklish circumstances. He must, therefore, be able to exercise good judgment as well as discretion. He must sometimes act with courage in apprehending lawbreakers. He must be completely dedicated to upholding the fish and game laws, without showing favor or partisanship. And he must, as the representative of the department, be diplomatic, possess some skill as a public speaker and writer, and have the kind of personality that enables him to get along with all classes of people. No small order. I have long considered the game warden to be grossly underpaid, considering the kind of person he must be and the job he must do.

A game warden in Montana starts with a salary of $738 a month and can advance to $973 a month. If he gets to be a warden sergeant he can make as much as $1,071 a month, and if he advances to a warden captain, he will make as much as $1,182 a month.

All states, Montana included, give intensive training in psychology and human relations to game wardens and other fish and game personnel who must frequently deal with the public, and sometimes on not such happy occasions. Special training in crime detection is also useful, since these workers may have to investigate illegal hunting or forest fire incendiarism.

Nibs Watt, Game Warden

M. J. ("Nibs") Watt was long a game warden in Montana. Prior to passing the qualifying test he was a hunting guide in the Yellowstone country of Montana. That gave him good practical experience he could apply to the job of warden.

"That qualifying test was a tough one," Nibs told me. "One of the questions was to name the young of the swan. Luckily I knew it was the cygnet, but knowing how to spell the word was even tougher."

Nibs was being modest. He passed the tough test with flying colors, being an avid student of all things connected with nature and the outdoors, and soon he was stationed as local game warden in one of the large counties of western Montana. That is when I came to know him, for I was appointed ex-officio game warden by the state of Montana in answer to their request to the Forest Service to furnish someone to assist Nibs during one of the fall hunting seasons. And that is when I came to respect game wardens and admire the work they do.

Nibs Watt and I visited with many big game hunters that fall. We stood by many hunting campfires, our presence never resented even though our badges were plain to see, because Nibs Watt had the right kind of personality for this work. An expert hunter himself, he could speak their language. He had learned well the large area of forests and mountains he patrolled, knew the habits of the big game animals that inhabited them, and could give good tips to those hunters, many of whom were from eastern states and inexperienced at hunting in this rugged country. Nibs was well liked by local hunters, too, because they had come to respect him as an impartial and fair upholder of the state fish and game laws.

He was relentless and fearless in bringing violators to justice. I remember one case that we investigated of a moose that had been illegally shot in a game preserve. Skillfully Nibs gathered what little evidence there was. Discreetly he made inquiries. In a matter of hours he had ferreted out a trail that led directly to the culprits.

In this and other cases we investigated Nibs always had to be sure of his facts, and he had to have overpowering evidence to gain a conviction. That is why game wardens today are often given FBI and other types of special training.

Nibs Watt, I learned, was also an expert in wildlife management. Often he received complaints from ranchers about beavers that were clogging irrigation canals by building dams in them. Nibs would set a live trap, an intricate wire-mesh affair, for the beavers, and when he caught a pair would transport them to some mountain stream where their dam building could do good rather than harm. For this, he had to know the habits of beavers, and he had to know the country where they could best survive.

Nibs Watt was a highly successful game warden. He served many years as a warden captain and went on to become chief game warden of all of Montana. Today he is retired and living in the same county where he got his start. Serving as game warden in that county today is a man Nibs helped to train.

THE PRIVATE SECTOR

Today there are increasing job opportunities for fish and game workers in private employment. Large landowning companies have fish and game resources that must be managed. Owners of large estates sometimes hire people to help them manage fish and game resources. The number of private fishing and hunting preserves is increasing, and these must be managed. Private consulting firms advise land and lake owners on fish and

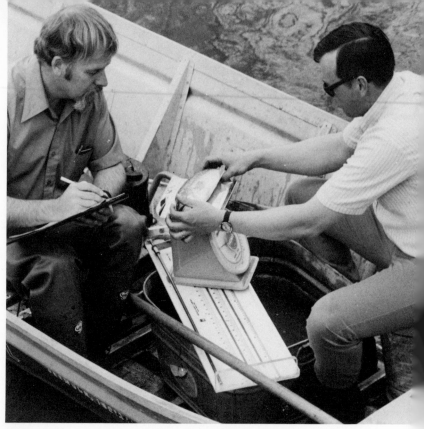

Gary Doxtater and Robert Johnson of Aquatic Control, Inc.

game matters. An example of the last is Aquatic Control, Inc., of Seymour, Indiana.

Gary Doxtater, Businessman-Biologist

Gary Doxtater, a fish and wildlife biologist, is president and principal biologist of Aquatic Control, Inc. He received his B.S. and M.A. degrees in zoology, specializing in fisheries, from Miami University, Oxford, Ohio.

During his graduate work, Doxtater received a research assistantship from the Ohio Division of Wildlife and was assigned to the Acton Lake limnological survey. In 1962 he was appointed a fisheries biologist by the Indiana Department of Natural Resources, Division of Fish and Wildlife.

He soon became chief biologist in charge of the Driftwood Experimental Station, conducting research on predator-prey relations, and he designed the state's first artificial northern pike spawning marsh. In 1964 he was promoted to supervisor of fish and wildlife, assisting the division director. In that important position he was responsible for the implementation of many statewide fish and wildlife programs.

But Gary Doxtater had gone into fish and wildlife work because he loved the outdoors. Now he was holding down an important position in his field, but one which required him to spend most of his time in an office. He looked about, reflected on his experience, and saw an opportunity. He spoke to C. J. Rust about it. Rust was head of a firm that built big dams. He agreed with Doxtater that expert help was needed in fish and wildlife management for the big reservoirs created by the dams. Together they formed Aquatic Control, Inc.

Aquatic Control, Inc., is kept very busy these days. The firm employs eighteen professionals and seven technicians. Implementation of the National Environmental Policy Act in 1969 has involved the company in ecological and environmental evaluation studies for various projects in the Middle West and the South. Gary Doxtater and his fellow specialists at Aquatic Control, Inc., provide a professional ecological approach to the control, preservation, and planning of the environment, particularly concerning waterways, reservoirs, lakes, and their adjacent lands. It is important work, and the need for it continues to grow.

Gary Doxtater thinks this private sector will become increasingly important in the employment picture for professionals and technicians in the field of fish and game management.

THE FOREST SERVICE

Wildlife management on the national forests and national grasslands primarily involves protection and improvement of habitat for both game and nongame species. An important and challenging part of the wildlife job in the Forest Service involves

the coordination of wildlife needs with other forest resources
activities.

Professional Jobs

An estimated 150 wildlife and fisheries biologists are employed by the Forest Service. Additional biologists have
branched out into regular administrative posts, such as national
forest supervisors.

The newly appointed biologist in the Forest Service may be
assigned work involving other resource activities on the ranger
district as part of his orientation and training. Subsequently he
can progress from wildlife project staff assistant to full staff officer in the forest supervisor offices to wildlife staff officer in the
regional offices and on to a staff position in the Washington
office. These positions range all the way up to GS-15.

John Mathisen, Forest Service Biologist

John Mathisen, staff biologist on the Chippewa National
Forest in Minnesota, has made a national reputation and
won honors for his work with the bald eagle, an endangered
species. John has succeeded in protecting over 100 active
eagle nests on his forest, even though the Chippewa is an
important timber and pulpwood forest. John also won a
national conservation award for his work in planning and
creating some 50,000 acres of wetlands for waterfowl and
northern pike propagation, work that is still going on.

John Mathisen's career is significant in several respects.
For one thing, he spent his youth in Chicago, and so is
living proof that a city boy can be successful in an outdoor
career. I have been afield with John and can testify to his
expertise in outdoor matters. He is knowledgeable not only
about wildlife, but about almost everything connected with
the outdoor country he works in. Perhaps this is because
besides his talents as a wildlife biologist he is skilled as a
writer and artist and is an expert photographer.

John is also a good teacher. As a result of his work, the
Chippewa National Forest has become something of a

A wildlife biologist examining trees cut for deer food. (*Wisconsin Natural Resources Department*)

"wildlife test tube," as he describes it. Students come to the Chippewa to learn from him. During the summer of 1974, for example, there were nine students on the forest doing research related to wildlife management needs.

John received a B.A. degree from Kendall College in Illinois in 1950. He then went to the University of Michigan, where he received a B.S. in 1954 and a M.S. in 1956. Following that, he worked as a district game supervisor for the Nebraska Game Commission from 1956 to 1962, when he came to the Chippewa National Forest as staff biologist.

Since then he has gained national recognition for his work, and has advanced in grade and pay. But the latter is not nearly so important to him as is the fact that he is doing the kind of work he is in the country where he wants to be.

Since John has trained many others to follow in his footsteps, I asked him what advice he could give others who might wish to do the same.

"A graduate degree is almost essential for the job-hunting biologist now," he says. "Jobs are in short supply, but this, as you know, fluctuates with time. With all the interest and concern over environmental matters, the biologist is being asked more and more to provide technical input and advice."

Nonprofessional Jobs

Biological technician jobs are also available in the Forest Service. The technicians work with the professionals and usually under the guidance of the professionals, with a heavy emphasis on field work.

Banding Canada geese. (*Wisconsin Natural Resources Department*)

A biological technician can frequently go as high as GS-9. No written test is necessary, but to qualify you must have successfully completed two academic years of study above the high school level in a junior or community college, specialized training school, technical institute, four-year college, or university. Your program of study must have included courses in the biological sciences. Many positions require at least twenty-four semester hours while others require as few as twelve.

In place of academic study you can substitute two years of technical experience in biological work, using appropriate equipment, methods, and practices. Two years of training and experience can be combined to qualify.

OTHER AGENCIES

Other agencies that hire fish and game management specialists are the federal land management agencies—the Bureau of Land Management, the Park Service. The Extension Service also needs this type of personnel, as do the Soil Conservation Service and the Bureau of Indian Affairs. The Environmental Protection Agency has hired many fish and game biologists in recent years to advise on fish and game matters. Fish and wildlife employees in the TVA work in the Division of Forestry, Fisheries and Wildlife Development.

An important employer of fishery and aquatic biologists is the National Marine Fisheries Service of the U.S. Department of Commerce. That agency administers programs to determine the consequences of the naturally varying environment and man's activities on living marine resources. Its national headquarters are at 3300 Whitehaven Parkway, Washington, D.C. 20240, but it has a great many regional centers for fisheries work and research. Examples are the Columbia River Fisheries Development Program based in Portland, Oregon; the Pribilof Islands Program in Seattle; the Southwest Fisheries Center at La Jolla, California; and the Atlantic Fishery Products Technology Center at Gloucester, Massachusetts. Employees of this agency are primarily concerned with the problems of commercial fisheries.

FUTURE PROSPECTS

Right now employment in fish and game management is tight, but the picture should become much brighter in the near future.

The Public Land Law Review Commission has recommended that "hunting, fishing, and other forms of use and enjoyment of resident wildlife and fish should be given equal consideration in federal public land programs, along with other uses of the public lands."

Acting on this recommendation, the U.S. Senate in July 1974 passed a bill giving the federal government authority to manage game, fish, and wildlife on certain federal lands. That the bill passed 87–0 shows the great sentiment that exists for it. It is under consideration by the House of Representatives as I write this and is almost certain to pass and become law. Such a law will increase management activities on land controlled by the Atomic Energy Commission, the National Aeronautics and Space Administration, the Forest Service, and the Bureau of Land Management, and this in turn will create many new fish and game jobs. The bill, as passed by the Senate, authorizes $23.5 million a year for the first five years of the program.

States, too, will hire more fish and game specialists because of a backlog of needs that has been building during recent years, due largely to presidential impoundment (now prohibited by law) of funds related to fish and game programs, such as the land and water conservation fund. Conservationists hope and expect to see this fund fully implemented in forthcoming years. As much as $300 million to $400 million annually will be granted to the states on a matching basis. This should bring about increased hiring of those who have the skills to do fish and game work.

More intensive use of public lands for fish and wildlife

enjoyment will require specific identification of areas that can be so used. This means more fish and wildlife specialists will be needed for land classification work.

Something else the Public Land Law Review Commission has recommended is "a general land use fee . . . for the recreational use of public lands." This is already in effect in some places. In West Virginia, for example, there is a cooperative agreement between the state and the Monongahela National Forest. A fee of $1 is charged for a sportsman's license to use the national forest for fishing and hunting. The fund thus created has enabled new fishing impoundments, wild turkey propagation, habitat improvement, and similar programs that have kept West Virginia an outstanding state for fishing and hunting. And this fund has created many fish and game jobs.

Charging fees for the use of lands and waters for hunting and fishing is also a growing practice with private landowners. On these private lands fish and game managers must often be employed to manage the fish and game resources, and organizations like Aquatic Control, Inc., will be increasingly called upon to conduct studies and give advice.

If you are eager to enter the field of wildlife management and are just beginning your schooling or are already in college, my advice is to get as broad an education as you possibly can. Learn to use words well, and don't become a narrow specialist, even if wildlife is your first love. Broaden your sights and you'll hit your target.

For more information contact:

American Fisheries Society
Fourth Floor Suite
1319 18th Street N.W.
Washington, D.C. 20036

American Institute of Biological Sciences, Inc.
3900 Wisconsin Avenue N.W.
Washington, D.C. 20016

North American Wildlife Foundation
709 Wire Building
Washington, D.C. 20005

Sport Fishing Institute
Suite 801
608 13th Street N.W.
Washington, D.C. 20005

Wildlife Management Institute
709 Wire Building
Washington, D.C. 20005

The Wildlife Society
Suite S-176
3900 Wisconsin Avenue N.W.
Washington, D.C. 20016

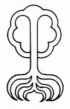

5: YOUR CAREER IN RANGE MANAGEMENT

Range management is an agricultural science—a science that needs to be much better implemented if we are to meet our future food needs.

Recently we have seen wide fluctuations in the supply of beef and other meat, along with continued high prices. How can range management help deal with this problem?

Our answer lies in experiments of the U.S. Forest Service at the Manitou Experimental Forest near Woodland Park, Colorado. There, careful studies proved that one square mile of range in excellent condition can produce more than 11,000 pounds of beef per year. The same area of range in good condition can produce some 7,300 pounds per year; a fair range, 4,600 pounds; a poor range, only 2,500 pounds or less.

It is the job of range management to upgrade poor and fair range into good range and to maintain as much excellent range as possible. It is a vital job, and one we are not yet accomplishing.

One of the problems is the decline in amount of grazing lands in the United States. Since 1880 we have lost some 300 million acres of range. Most of that acreage has been converted to cropland. In the last few years wheat acreage has greatly increased to meet world demands on American wheat plus our own domestic demands. Moreover, the rangeland that has gone into cultivation has been the best, leaving the poorer land for continued grazing. This makes the job of range management even more difficult and even more necessary.

The United States still has approximately 1 billion acres of grazing land, 630 million acres of which are permanent grasslands, while 320 million acres are mixed grasslands and forest, much of it high country that can be grazed only part of the year. The remainder includes cropland and planted fields that are pastured by livestock.

The original American grasslands were truly marvelous. They made up about two fifths of the entire acreage of the country and gave sustenance to millions of grazing animals on which the Indians depended for their survival.

Overgrazing and bad management of the range, as well as conversion of much of the range into cropland, have left us very little rangeland in its original condition. And range management science is relatively new. We are still learning about it, and we have yet to apply widely the knowledge we do have.

A healthy range is needed not only to produce sufficient meat, but also to maintain the health of the land itself. Many people argue that crop production is the best possible use of land for meeting the world's food needs, and it is true that raising wheat and other edible grains is a more direct way of feeding people and that an acre of cropland will feed more people than an acre of rangeland. But not all rangeland can be converted

into cropland. Most conservationists agree that too much rangeland has already been so converted, and that this has led to
grave land problems, particularly in times of drought. The dust
storms of the 1930s resulted from the plowing of the rangelands
of the West.

Most rangeland today occurs west of the 100th meridian. It
is there that most range management workers will be employed.
At one time this was all open range. Much of it is still public
domain, owned by all the people, and administered by such
agencies as the Bureau of Land Management and the Forest
Service. Much of it is broken up into ranches of various sizes,
from those encompassing a few hundred acres to those measured
in square miles. Becoming increasingly important in recent years
are the irrigated pasturelands, especially in the mountain valleys,
where reclamation projects have made otherwise arid lands fer-
tile with grasses that are highly productive for cattle and sheep
raising. More haylands are being irrigated, too, to assure adequate winter feed for the meat-producing animals. Pasture grazing can be a science itself, as can hayland irrigation.

DEVELOPMENT OF RANGE MANAGEMENT

The range industry in America goes back many years. The
earliest explorers, including Leif Ericson, brought animals with
them to graze and furnish an assured meat supply. Coronado, in
1540, was probably the first to establish grazing in a big way,
bringing cattle, sheep, and horses into the American Southwest.
Some of these animals escaped and were the progenitors of wild
herds, especially the horses, which the Indians learned to capture
and use.

By the time the immigrants began moving across the West
to Oregon and California in the middle of the nineteenth century, cattle, sheep, and horses were common throughout the
United States, and during the rest of that century there was a
vast increase of grazing livestock on the western ranges.

Little care was given to the land itself. The region was so lush no one dreamed it could be overgrazed. But when severe winters set in and periods of drought came, it became obvious that the range had suffered from overgrazing. Ranches had to become larger and larger to remain even marginally profitable. Many original homesteads were lost, and their former owners had to find other ways of making a living, often by going to work for a richer, more successful neighbor. Others just moved on, hoping for better luck in another place. Much of the history of the West is a history of range abuse. No real effort was made to practice good range management until well into the present century.

The creation of the Forest Service in the U.S. Department of Agriculture was the turning point for range conservation in America. Gifford Pinchot, chief forester, recognized grazing as a legitimate use of the national forests, but at the same time he was determined to ensure proper use. To that end he hired Albert F. Potter, a pioneer Arizona stockman, as his assistant in charge of range management for the Forest Service.

Potter, with the backing of Pinchot, worked out grazing policies and regulations that were remarkable for the time, and were democratic in principle, in keeping with Pinchot's philosophy of public land management. These Forest Service policies established that priority in the use of national forest range would be given to those already using the range, with necessary changes in livestock numbers or herd management to be made gradually so as not to work a hardship on the user; the small operator would be favored over the large; conservation and improvement work would be undertaken; range use would be compatible with other aspects of good forest management; and the stockmen would have a voice in the formulation of management rules.

In keeping with these policies, permits were issued to leasers of national forest range. The permits spelled out not only how many animals could be grazed, but also for how long a time—

when they could be turned out on the range in the spring, and when they would have to be brought in in the fall. To work out equitable agreements as well as to solve other range problems, the Forest Service encouraged the organization of local stockmen's associations, with rangers playing an active role. The 800 associations formed helped keep many small stockmen in business who otherwise could not have survived.

The national forests, however, constituted only a portion of the public domain. An even larger portion was left unmanaged until 1934, when the Taylor Grazing Act was passed and the Grazing Service was established. Then, in 1946, the Grazing Service was merged with the General Land Office and became the Bureau of Land Management. What were known as Taylor grazing lands became BLM lands, the largest block of public lands in the United States.

The purpose of the Taylor Grazing Act was "to stop injury to the public grazing lands by preventing overgrazing and soil deterioration, to provide for their orderly use, improvement, and development, to stabilize the livestock industry dependent upon the public range, and for other purposes." Those "other purposes" include such multiple uses as are found on the national forests, with emphasis increasingly given to recreation and wildlife management.

The Taylor Grazing Act also set up grazing districts, modeled on the earlier Forest Service stockmen's associations, with an advisory board of local stockmen in each district and the issuance of permits for grazing along with rules and regulations worked out locally.

Another important piece of legislation at this same time was the Wheeler-Howard Act of 1934, also known as the Indian Reformation Act in the Bureau of Indian Affairs. Both the Grazing Service (now BLM) and the Indian bureau were placed in the Department of the Interior. The Wheeler-Howard Act provided for the conservation and development of the land resources on the various Indian reservations. The large areas of range on these reservations can now be grazed only on an allotment basis with specified stocking and fee systems.

States with large areas of range have set up grazing rules and regulations, permitting livestock producers to graze on state lands. And when the Soil Conservation Service was established in the 1930s, it served as an advisory agency to grazers and hired many range management specialists.

About that time, too, range management became a recognized educational discipline, and colleges and universities in the western states began offering academic degrees in the subject. In 1960 the Range Management Education Council was established "to promote high standards in the teaching of range management . . . and in other ways to foster wider understanding of the problems of range education."

The Society of Range Management was created in 1947 "to advance the science and art of grazing land management, to promote progress in conservation and sustained use of forage, soil and water resources, to stimulate discussion and understanding of range and pasture problems, to provide a medium of exchange of ideas and facts among members and with allied scientists, and to encourage professional improvement of members."

Range management is, then, one of the newest of the agricultural sciences. Despite its youth, it has accomplished much notable work—reclaiming unproductive rangeland and pastureland, better fencing, developing of stock-watering facilities, and the advancement of fertilization practices. But its work has only begun. It is a profession with great potential.

WORKING IN RANGE MANAGEMENT

RANGE MANAGER

In 1968, an estimated 4,000 professional range managers were employed in the United States. The majority were employed by federal government agencies, primarily the Forest Service and the Soil Conservation Service of the Department of

Through range management, the grazing capacity of this restored land has increased at least four times over what it was. (*U.S. Forest Service*)

Agriculture, and the Bureau of Land Management of the Department of the Interior. State governments also employed significant numbers of range managers.

Range managers are employed by privately owned livestock ranches. Some are in business for themselves as managers of their own land. Some are self-employed consultants or are employed by consulting firms. Others work for manufacturing, sales, and service enterprises, and for banks and real estate firms that need rangeland appraisals. Colleges and universities employ range managers in teaching and research positions.

Training leading to a bachelor's degree with a major in range management was offered in 1968 by twenty-five colleges and universities, mainly in western and southwestern states. Twenty-three of these schools also grant a master's degree, and fifteen award a doctorate.

The essential courses for a degree in range management are botany, plant ecology, plant physiology, zoology, animal husbandry, soils, chemistry, mathematics, and specialized courses in range management, such as identification and characteristics

Ranger F. R. ("Doc") Cornell counting cattle entering a grazing allotment in the Lewis and Clark National Forest. (*U.S. Forest Service*)

of range plants, range improvement, and range sampling and inventory techniques. Desirable elective courses include economics, statistical methods, physics, geology, watershed management, wildlife management, surveying, and forage crops.

Federal agencies hire many college juniors and seniors for summer jobs in range management. This experience helps qualify students for permanent positions as range managers when they complete college.

Because a range manager must meet and deal with other people, individually or in groups, he should be able to communicate his ideas effectively, both in writing and speaking. Many jobs require the stamina to perform vigorous physical activity and the willingness to work in arid and sparsely populated areas.

Digging trenches and laying pipe to bring water for stock into a range area previously unused because of lack of water. (*U.S. Forest Service*)

John Forsman, Range Manager

I became acquainted with John Forsman soon after he graduated from the Montana University School of Forestry with a major in range management. He had gone to work as an assistant ranger on the Stevensville Ranger District of the Bitterroot National Forest. This is in western Montana, where there are more mountains with forests and timber than flat grazing lands. John loved the country, but he had been raised on a ranch in eastern Montana and loved range management work most of all. His career was interrupted by World War II, when he served his country in the armed services. In 1945, back from the war, he was appointed chief of party for range survey in the Division of Range and Wildlife Management in Region I of the Forest Service, with headquarters in Missoula, Montana. It should be mentioned here that range management and wildlife management are often combined disciplines in the Forest Service, and John Forsman had studied wildlife management in college. This was to be of value to him in his career. In 1947 he became district ranger of the Musselshell District on the Lewis and Clark National Forest in Montana, a forest with a lot of rangeland and grazing. John was now doing the work he loved most. In 1954 he was appointed assistant forest supervisor in charge of range and wildlife management on the Custer National Forest in Montana, another heavy rangeland forest. In 1958 he became forest supervisor of the Custer, serving in that key post for five years, when he was called to the Washington, D.C., headquarters to serve as assistant director of the Division of Range Management. And in 1967 he became assistant regional forester, in charge of the Division of Range and Wildlife Management for the Pacific Northwest Region of the Forest Service, a job he still holds.

John Forsman is in charge of range and wildlife management for nineteen national forests, including forests in eastern Oregon and Washington that have a great deal of rangeland to administer. The fact that he is responsible for both range and wildlife management on these forests proves how closely related the two fields are, and how a man like Forsman can in his career gain the necessary experience to manage both these important resources on such key public lands.

I asked John Forsman what were the chances for young people in range management.

"Seriously," he said, "I believe that in the future federal land managing agencies such as the Forest Service will have greater need for the technical services of range scientists and wildlife biologists. The range and wildlife resources are becoming more important to the public. So far as range management is concerned, I see a greater demand for range forage for livestock in the future than we have had in the past. Indications are that demand for meat—beef particularly—will continue to increase if prices can be kept reasonable. Current meat production systems require energy using machines to raise feed grains. Under the present feed shortage, I believe there will be a shift from feed grain to range forage for livestock production especially since the nation's ranges have the capacity to produce the additional forage needed. A real opportunity exists for USDA to make a substantial contribution through intensification of range programs on the national forests and on associated private lands."

Range aid positions are available in government agencies for those who do not have college degrees. Range aids perform various tasks in connection with the management, conservation, development, utilization, and protection of rangeland for the continuous production of forage and related range resources utilized by livestock or big game. Grade schedules are generally from GS-1 through GS-4.

Technicians are also employed, increasingly so, and they can advance to grade GS-12. Technicians should have a combination of experience plus at least two years of vocational training in a technical school. Technicians relieve range managers of many of the outdoor chores, and in some cases even serve as range managers themselves. Their duties include inventorying, analyzing, improving, protecting, utilizing, and managing the natural resources of rangelands and related grazing lands; regulating grazing on public rangelands; developing cooperative relations with range users; assisting landowners to plan and apply range conservation programs; developing technical standards and specifications; conducting research on the principles underlying rangeland management; and developing new or improved instruments and techniques.

EMPLOYMENT OPPORTUNITIES

THE FOREST SERVICE

Range conservationists in the Forest Service are responsible for helping provide nationwide leadership in forest range conservation, development, and utilization. Their work centers are on the national forests and national grasslands, where they develop the 106-million-acre range environment to its potential and manage it properly.

Grazing national forestlands in thirty-eight states are 7 million cattle and sheep owned by 20,000 rancher-farmers. Several million browsing elk, deer, and other wildlife also inhabit these lands. The ranges also support recreational use.

A typical day might find the Forest Service range conservationist in the field making a range allotment analysis of one of the thousands of national forest grazing allotments, developing plans for rehabilitating depleted range, supervising construction of water developments and fences, developing a rest-rotation system of grazing, or making impact studies to determine the suitability, condition, and trend of the vegetation and soil and the grazing capacity of the various management units. Another day might find him tabulating sheep, tagging or marking cattle as they enter the national forest, or meeting with a stockmen's association or individual stockmen to discuss management plans.

At present, over 600 persons with training in range management are employed by the Forest Service. Each year the Forest Service hires around 50 college graduates with a background in range management. Entrance levels are at grades GS-5 to GS-7, depending on an individual's qualifications and experience. Promotions are based on ability and merit, with the initial promotion usually following satisfactory completion of a year's service. Range management careers in the Forest Service extend through the GS-15 level.

The Forest Service also conducts range management research at its numerous forest and range experiment stations and in the field on national forests and national grasslands. Researchers have at least the master's degree, and in many cases the doctorate, in range management science.

The Forest Service manages 155 national forests, 19 national grasslands, and 19 land utilization projects, containing 187 million acres, and forage resources are found on all these units.

Grazing is allowed on ranges within the national forests themselves, as well as on the 3.8 million acres of national grasslands.

THE BUREAU OF LAND MANAGEMENT

The BLM is a large employer of range management specialists, since it has over 400 million acres of range resources.

As a professional range manager with the bureau, you have an opportunity to participate in a progressive range management and administration program that utilizes some of the latest scientific principles and practices. Major emphasis is given to range conditions as the key to successful multiple use of bureau lands. Like the Forest Service, the BLM is committed to such management by congressional legislation.

Because the bureau's rangelands are managed on a multiple-use basis, you become experienced in closely related activities—wildlife and watershed management, land classification, mineral resources, forest management, and recreation. Through experience in these various activities and association with other professional employees, you gain a broad background of experience and develop to full professional stature in the field of range management and resource conservation.

A small number of beginning professionals recently graduated from college are brought into the bureau each year at grades GS-5 and GS-7. The bureau's primary employment opportunities are in Alaska, Arizona, California, Colorado, Idaho, Montana, Nevada, Oregon, Utah, Washington, and Wyoming.

THE SOIL CONSERVATION SERVICE

SCS range conservationists help ranchers and other range users to determine the suitability of their land for production of native forage and other plants for livestock, wildlife, and recreation and to develop conservation plans to improve the condition of their ranges. They give on-site technical assistance to landowners concerning range inventories, proper forage utilization, reseeding, brush control, water development, and grazing system. Qualifications include a college degree with major study in range management or range conservation with specified courses outlined in the examination announcement for this position.

THE BUREAU OF INDIAN AFFAIRS

The BIA also hires range conservationists to assist in the management of some 39 million acres held in trust for the Indians. You do not have to be an Indian to work for this bureau, but if you are a native American you should look into the possibilities for employment as a range management specialist on your tribal lands.

OTHER AGENCIES

In the Department of Agriculture, range management specialists are needed in the Agricultural Research Service, the Agricultural Stabilization and Conservation Service, the Cooperative State Research Service, and the Extension Service.

The military services that manage land—the air force, army, and navy—need range management specialists to advise on management plans.

The Fish and Wildlife Service of the Department of the Interior hires range management specialists because many of the national wildlife refuges are located in the grassland areas of the prairie states and the West, are primarily ranges, and are even often called that. Examples are the Niobrara Refuge in Nebraska, where the famous Texas longhorn cattle roam free on a vast grassland; the Charles Russell Range in Montana, which is managed as an example of early, good range conditions; and the National Bison Range, also in Montana.

The Park Service of the Department of the Interior also needs range management specialists, since many of the national parks and monuments contain large areas of grassland that must be carefully managed to sustain wild animal populations.

FUTURE PROSPECTS

Employment opportunities for graduates with degrees in range management are expected to be good through the next decade at least. The demand will be especially great for well-qualified persons with advanced degrees who can fill research and teaching positions.

Opportunities will probably be best in federal agencies. Favorable opportunities also are expected in private industry, since range livestock producers and private timber operators are hiring increasing numbers of range managers to improve their range holdings. A few openings are expected in developing countries of the Middle East, Africa, and South America, where range managers are needed to give technical assistance.

Among the major factors underlying the anticipated increase in demand for range managers are population growth, increasing per capita consumption of animal products, and the growing use of rangelands for hunting and other recreational activities. Many openings are expected because of more intensive management of range resources due to increasing emphasis on multiple use of rangelands. Range managers will be needed to help rehabilitate deteriorated rangelands, improve semiarid lands, and deal with watershed problems.

For more information contact:

National Association of Conservation Districts
1025 Vermont Avenue N.W.
Washington, D.C. 20005

Society for Range Management
2120 South Birch Street
Denver, Colorado 80222

6: YOUR CAREER IN OUTDOOR ENGINEERING AND ENVIRONMENT MANAGEMENT

Not long ago engineers were a dime a dozen. Young men and women were discouraged from embarking on engineering careers. Enrollments fell off in engineering schools.

Today the very opposite is the case. An engineering graduate can have his pick of well-paying jobs. Graduates are often flown at company expense to be interviewed.

There is a moral to this: any type of career that is eminently useful can only be tight for a short time. Professional disciplines such as engineering never cease to advance, and such advances bring an increased need for well-educated practitioners.

WHAT IS OUTDOOR ENGINEERING?

This chapter concerns the kind of engineering that is conducted outdoors and that has to do with conservation of natural resources—outdoor construction work, landscape architecture, and environmental engineering. These are professional jobs. Also discussed is the engineering technician, whose role is becoming increasingly important.

Because of our growing concern for the environment, the engineer today more than ever before needs a good knowledge of the physical laws of nature so that he can apply the mechanical properties of the materials he works with. He must also be able to work with people, and this requires a good background in the humanities and the social sciences. The time has long since passed when the engineer could be a narrow specialist narrowly trained.

The engineering specialty most specifically adapted to work outdoors is civil engineering—planning, designing, and supervising the construction of such improvements as roads, buildings, dams, trails, campgrounds, boat launching ramps, sanitary facilities, and bridges. Civil engineering can include the work that goes into providing transportation facilities, controlling water, providing shelter, and maintaining a suitable environment.

Many government and private agencies involved with improving, protecting, and utilizing outdoor natural resources need civil engineers. The minimum requirement for most qualified professionals is a bachelor's degree in civil engineering. And for the kind of engineering we are referring to here, you should have a love for the outdoors and for roughing it, for that is where and how you will be spending a good part of your time. For this reason, until recent years civil engineering has been a field dominated by men. But these days more and more women are becoming civil engineers.

WORKING FOR THE FOREST SERVICE

ENGINEERS

The Forest Service is currently engaged in an extensive development and improvement program on the 155 national forests.

Expansion of this program is expected to continue for many years.

To implement this improvement program, the Forest Service needs a skilled engineering staff. The increasing volume of work also indicates that Forest Service engineers will have better than normal opportunities to advance to more responsible and better paid positions. Engineers have been placed in charge of Forest Service regions and have become deputy chiefs in the organization.

The largest engineering activity in the Forest Service is the design and construction of the new roads and bridges needed to harvest timber and to provide access for national forest users, including the many recreationists. In past years the Forest Service has averaged over 6,000 miles of new road each year. Many old roads have had to be improved to accommodate heavier equipment and increased traffic. Thanks to the Environmental Policy Act of 1969, these roads must today be planned so as to do the least amount of environmental damage.

This makes road building in the Forest Service a complex business. It is a challenge to the professional ability of the most capable engineers. The major portion of the new mileage now being built lies in rugged mountain terrain. In such a setting each new mile presents new problems.

Road building is only one phase of the work done by Forest Service civil engineers. As road construction makes more areas accessible, other improvements must follow. Administrative structures, warehouses, dormitories, family housing, visitor information centers, dams, campgrounds, water and sanitation facilities must be designed and built. Each location is different, and previously developed plans must be modified or replaced to meet different requirements. This precludes extensive use of standard plans and requires the engineer on each job to work out his own solutions.

Forest Service engineering is organized to provide the young engineer with the opportunity to develop a broad background of training and experience. Each of the 155 national forests has its own engineering staff, directed by a forest engineer. The engineers assigned to the forest are responsible for the complete engineering job, although bridges, buildings, and other complex structures are usually designed at the regional offices.

The Forest Service also uses civil engineers in a number of specialized fields. Among these are cadastral (ownership) surveys, topographical surveys and map making, materials testing, watershed protection, soils classification, and photogrammetry. Some graduates begin their professional engineering careers in one of these specialized fields. Others prefer to gain one or two years of general field engineering experience before transferring into one of the specialties.

Engineers usually enter the Forest Service at the GS-5 or GS-7 level, depending on their qualifications and experience. Engineering careers in the Forest Service extend through GS-16.

LANDSCAPE ARCHITECTS

The Forest Service is the largest single employer of landscape architects in the country. This type of professional has long found employment in the Forest Service, but thanks again to the Environmental Policy Act of 1969, the organization has become increasingly concerned with making its engineering activity conform to the protection and health needs of the environment, and the landscape architect plays an important role in this work. Today nearly every national forest has a landscape architect on its staff.

Landscape architects enter the Forest Service at the GS-5 and GS-7 levels. A degree in landscape architecture or landscape design is a civil service requisite. Those with courses or experience in surveying, conservation, civil engineering, public speaking, and writing are particularly needed for Forest Service positions. Entrance at the GS-7 level is possible if the applicant has a master's degree, maintained a B average or better in col-

Rock drilling and powder setting for construction of a timber road in the Bitterroot National Forest. (*U.S. Forest Service*)

lege, graduated in the upper 25 percent of his class, qualified for an accredited honor society, or attained other specified scholastic levels. Graduate study, advanced degrees, or professional experience may qualify you for entrance at an even higher level.

ENGINEERING AIDS AND TECHNICIANS

Nonprofessionals are important in Forest Service outdoor engineering. An engineer's road design for a national forest is useless without a corps of unskilled, skilled, and supervisory workers to build the road. The Forest Service, like any other large organization, needs employees with different levels of skills and functions who can cooperate harmoniously.

In the Forest Service (as well as other such agencies), technicians have taken over from the professional engineer such responsible and difficult jobs as supervising on-the-ground operations in road and other types of construction that require practical skills and experience.

What is true of the technician is also true of the aid. No organization can exist without people who can get the basic, preliminary work done. The Forest Service is fortunate in having hardworking aids who not only get the job done, but enjoy doing it. In its early days the Forest Service relied heavily on the woodsman's skills of local residents, who possessed much practical knowledge about building and maintaining national forest improvements. These capable men often advanced to high positions in the organization. Even today such advancement is possible for nonprofessionals who have developed the requisite skills in getting the job done.

Survey work on Slate Pass in the state of Washington. (*U.S. Department of the Interior, Geological Survey*)

Aids work at a variety of engineering tasks that help both the technician and professional. They serve on a road survey crew as rodmen, rear or head chainmen, notekeepers, or level instrument men. These survey crews on national forests generally begin work in the spring, spending weeks in the field gathering data for construction work, often far from town. The work continues into the fall as long as weather permits.

Skilled workers, many of them, are hired by the Forest Service for engineering jobs on the national forests. Needed are carpenters, stonemasons, bulldozer and road grader operators, and others experienced in various crafts and trades. The Forest Service pays prevailing local wage rates for this skilled help. In addition the organization hires many laborers to assist in getting the engineering jobs done. Again local prevailing wage rates are paid.

Technicians usually begin at the GS-5 level. The appropriate job title is engineering and survey technician. Candidates for technician positions must have a minimum of two years of general experience and one year of specialized experience. Substituting high school or other education for parts of the general and specialized experience requirements is permitted.

GS-2 or GS-3 is the beginning grade for engineering aids and surveying aids. Candidates for aid positions must have at least six months of general experience for the GS-2 grade, and one year of general experience for the GS-3 grade. In some cases, high school graduation may be substituted for the six months of general experience.

There are some engineering positions in the Forest Service to which physically handicapped persons can be assigned, and whenever possible, these assignments are made.

Engineering Technician in the Forest Service

Some years ago when I was doing fire control work for the Forest Service, a letter came to me from a young woman who was seeking employment. I suppose it was put on my

Glen Canyon Dam construction. (*U.S. Department of the Interior, Bureau of Reclamation*)

desk because she was applying for a fire control job. She had worked one season as a fire lookout on another national forest. I was impressed by her well-written letter. She had gone several years to college, studying forestry but with heavy emphasis on engineering. At that time it was unusual for a woman to enter such a field.

After consulting with the administration officer, I suggested she come in for a personal interview, since she lived fairly close. She did, and she was hired.

Today that same woman has nearly fifteen years of experience as a skilled engineering technician on that same national forest. An outdoor enthusiast, she has been able to combine drafting and survey and design with frequent outdoor trips in some of the best country in the United States. She draws a good salary and is highly respected for her work. She is doing exactly what she wanted to do.

EMPLOYMENT OPPORTUNITIES OUTSIDE THE FOREST SERVICE

THE ARMY CORPS OF ENGINEERS

The Army Corps of Engineers is the largest engineering organization in the free world, and hence hires more engineers than any other single organization. And like the Forest Service and other government agencies, it hires many associated professionals besides civil engineers—architects, environmentalists, and ecologists, for example.

The Army Corps of Engineers is quietly revolutionizing its mission, reflecting a new era of concern over the quality of life in America. It faces the challenge of enhancing this quality of life by balancing the development of our water resources with the protection of our natural environment.

In the past, conservationists have often been at odds with the Corps of Engineers because of the corps' propensity to build huge dams and flood lovely river valleys. Even so, fair-minded conservationists give the corps credit for doing yeoman work in making our river systems safer and more feasible for water transportation and the riparian lands safer from the danger of floods. Without the work of the Corps of Engineers, many river and harbor cities, such as New Orleans, could scarcely exist today.

The corps seeks people with the broadest possible range of backgrounds. The wider your interests, the better. The more you bring to the corps, the more career opportunities you will have. Among major disciplines involved in corps work are engineering, architecture, landscape architecture, geology, ecology, hydrology, urban planning, cartography, geodesy, and geography.

In the corps you will have many opportunities to rise above a narrow specialty or sphere of interest if you wish to do so. And employees of the Corps of Engineers enjoy all the advantages provided under the federal civil service.

During a typical year the corps acquires over 10,000 tracts of land at a cost in excess of $100 million and manages over 37 million acres of land that cost the government more than $40 billion. It administers approximately 50,000 leases from private enterprise and over 35,000 outgrants that allow temporary use of federal lands. The corps arranges for the disposal of all excess real property of the army and air force and the other federal agencies it serves. These disposals average 1,500 units a year, with an original cost of approximately $200 million.

As the world's foremost military mapping agency, the U.S. Army Topographic Command of the Corps of Engineers pursues and manages operation, research, and development programs in geodesy, mapping and charting, geography, and military intelligence. More than 3,300 civilian employees train and work at this command's headquarters near the nation's capital; another 900 staff its field offices, and still others are on assignment to some of the fifty-seven foreign nations with which working agreements are maintained. While the mission of this command is primarily guided by military and defense requirements, a wide variety of environmental research programs guarantees your involvement in the latest advancements in many fields.

Because of the nature of the U.S. Army Topographic Command's mission, its career opportunities are somewhat different from those of other corps installations. There are outstanding opportunities available to science graduates with course work in astronomy, cartography, electronics engineering science, forest mensuration, geodesy, geophysics, mathematics, navigation, oceanography, optics, photogrammetry, physics, and surveying.

The Geological Survey, an arm of the U.S. Department of the Interior, is the principal federal agency concerned with preparing accurate maps of the physical features of the country and providing scientific information essential to the development of the nation's land, mineral, and water resources. It is recognized as one of the world's foremost research organizations in the earth sciences.

The survey makes topographical maps, hydrological maps, geological maps, and a variety of outline maps. It studies the earth's processes that may be hazardous to man and his works. It develops new prospecting techniques. It studies the natural processes that form deposits of valuable minerals. It takes a continuing inventory of the nation's water resources. It classifies federally owned lands for mineral and waterpower potential. It supervises mining and oil and gas development on federal and Indian lands. It conducts fundamental research in topography, geology, hydrology, geochemistry, geophysics, and related sciences. It publishes maps and reports to make the results of these investigations available to the public.

One of the most familiar products of the Geological Survey is the topographical or contour map. One of the major goals of the survey is the preparation and maintenance of a series of topographical maps that cover the entire United States and its possessions.

Geological Survey work requires the concerted efforts of

many kinds of scientists, engineers, and technical assistants. The work of the survey is divided among four operating divisions: topographical, geological, water resources, and conservation.

Modern map making requires teamwork among field survey engineers, photogrammetry specialists who compile and check the maps, and skilled cartographers who scribe and edit the final map manuscripts.

Because a considerable part of the country is still inadequately mapped, the Topographic Division maps those areas having the highest priority for military and civil needs. Field survey parties work throughout the year on assignments in all parts of the nation and Antarctica. Photogrammetric operations and map finishing are done in facilities in Reston, Virginia; Rolla, Missouri; Denver, Colorado; and Menlo Park, California.

Engineering geology is the application of all branches of geological knowledge to the interpretation of geological conditions that affect the safety, efficiency, and economy of engineering works. It is an important and varied field, for most of man's large scale construction remains on the surface or within the earth. Where structures are placed and how they are designed, built, and maintained depends in part on the nature and relations of the surrounding rocks and soils.

Fitting a structure to its geological environment begins with preliminary surveys and site selection, but the need for geological information continues in the design, construction, and maintenance of a structure. The geologist works closely with the engineer and advises him of the properties and distribution of the geological materials.

Paul Barton, Geologist

Paul Barton is a geologist who has made a successful career with the Geological Survey. Barton was employed by the survey on an intermittent basis in 1952 and 1953 after he had obtained an A.B. degree in geology from Pennsylvania State College. He continued postgraduate work and was awarded the Ph.D. degree from Columbia University in

1955. He joined the survey as a permanent employee that same year.

Barton's work with the survey has consisted mainly of research in the application of methods and theory of physical chemistry to the solution of geological problems. He has also conducted original research in mineralogy and petrology to find out how ore deposits are formed. He has authored and coauthored many significant technical papers and publications, and he has received numerous honors for his work, including outstanding performance ratings in 1958 and 1965, and the interior department's meritorious service award.

THE NATIONAL PARK SERVICE

The National Park Service hires a good number of engineers as well as engineering aids and technicians. You can qualify as a student assistant in the Park Service if you are studying architecture, engineering, or landscape architecture. This will give you, during the summer, on-the-job training in field surveys, planning design, and construction supervision. Student assistants work out of the service center in Denver, Colorado. To qualify you must be a student attending an accredited college pursuing a course related to one of these professional fields. For a GS-3 position, you must have completed one year of study; for GS-4, two years. Applicants for engineer and architect positions also must qualify in the summer employment examination conducted by the Civil Service Commission. Your school guidance counseling office can give you information on this.

Engineers have long been important in national park administration and development. Some of them have become well known. Hiram M. Chittenden, for example, who built some of the early roads and bridges in Yellowstone, became famous as a historian-writer of the West. Some of the most beautiful roads, bridges, and buildings in the country are to be found in the national parks and monuments.

The Fish and Wildlife Service employs approximately fifty engineers in the fields of civil, general, and hydraulic engineering and construction. They plan, design, and construct facilities for wildlife refuges and fish hatcheries. Because the regional offices are directly responsible for the program, employment inquiries should be directed to those offices. The service also employs skilled and semiskilled workers for engineering work.

The Bureau of Reclamation, discussed at length in Chapter 3, hires many different kinds of engineers and engineering aids and technicians.

Other federal agencies—the Bureau of Indian Affairs, the Bureau of Land Management, and the Environmental Protection Agency—hire people with engineering skills and education.

The Tennessee Valley Authority, a quasi-government agency, is another job source.

State agencies employ large numbers of civil and construction engineers in a wide range of positions that are similar to positions in private industry.

WHAT IS ENVIRONMENTAL ENGINEERING?

A new and expanding field is environmental engineering. State departments of natural resources are hiring increasing numbers of environmental engineers. Here is the class description for environmental engineer 1 in the Wisconsin department:

> *This is beginning level work in the field of environmental engineering duties to learn the standard procedures and practices employed in all phases of environmental health sanitation and environmental protection engineering activi-*

*ties. Work is performed under immediate supervision and
reviewed through the observation of performance and the
discussion of assignments to evaluate professional development.*

Increasingly, environmental engineers are being hired by
the many federal agencies and by private industry as well. A
young friend of mine who graduated as an environmental engineer is now employed by a leading engineering consulting firm,
helping to evaluate site proposals for electric power generating
plants.

Many counties, including rural counties, hire environmental
engineers and similarly qualified people to serve as county sani-
tarians, inspecting facilities and upholding laws for health and
related concerns.

Some of these jobs pay very well. Wisconsin pays beginning
environmental engineers $868 a month. Periodic increases can
raise monthly pay to $1,341. From there the employee can go on
to better paying administrative jobs.

Environmental engineers are called upon to do a wide variety of work. They investigate and inspect public water supply
systems, sewage collection systems, and industrial waste treatment facilities. They collect samples for bacteriological, chemical, and biological analysis and perform laboratory analyses.
They investigate water and air pollution. They conduct environmental surveys and write reports on their findings.

A number of colleges and universities grant degrees in environmental engineering. Notable among these are the University
of Denver, the University of Houston, Vanderbilt University, and
Columbia University.

Ecology is a good area for the biologically inclined student
to investigate. Ecology embraces not only the biological sciences,
but also chemistry, physics, astronomy, and metallurgy.

Today educational institutions are giving students more of
an opportunity to major in ecology. Some examples are San

Diego State College, which has a program in systems ecology leading to a B.S. degree; the University of Wisconsin at Green Bay, which has a College of Environmental Sciences focusing on ecology; Rutgers University in New Jersey, with a Department of Environmental Sciences that teaches the student about "the protection of man and his environment against unwarranted assaults"; Middlebury College in Vermont, which offers an environmental studies program that enables the student to gain a B.A. in ecology; Washington State University at Pullman, which grants both the B.S. and M.S. for studies emphasizing environmental biology.

FUTURE PROSPECTS

Engineers of all types are in demand now and will no doubt continue to be in demand. The Tennessee Valley Authority, for example, is planning and building additional multipurpose river development projects as well as hydro, conventional fuel, and nuclear power plants. The power requirements of the region are growing at the rate of more than 1 million kilowatts a year, requiring the annual addition of about $200 million in new generation and transmission facilities. These will be designed and constructed by the TVA's own engineering forces.

Many other agencies and private utility companies will be hiring increasing numbers of engineers, aids, and technicians to meet public demands for energy, recreation facilities, and the like. The work of the Environmental Protection Agency will undoubtedly broaden and the EPA will need many more people trained in the environmental sciences. States are forming their own environmental protection agencies, and engineers will be needed to set and enforce state standards on air and water pollution, as well as on land degradation, such as that caused by strip mining.

The U.S. Department of Labor expects 65,000 job openings for engineers each year, at least through the 1970s. In the environmental field alone there is now a deficit of over 50,000 professionals, and this is expected to increase to over 100,000 by 1980.

Ecology is a small but rapidly growing field. It and environment management may be the top growth industry by the end of this decade.

For more information contact:

American Society of Landscape Architects
1750 Old Meadow Road
McLean, Virginia 22101

Ecological Society of America
c/o Secretary Dr. Frank McCormick
Department of Botany
University of North Carolina
Chapel Hill, North Carolina 27514

Environmental Research Institute
Box 156
Moose, Wyoming 83012

International Institute for Environmental Affairs
United Nations Plaza
345 East 46th Street
New York, New York 10017

John Muir Institute for Environmental Studies
1079 Mills Tower
San Francisco, California 94104

Association of Conservation Engineers
c/o Secretary-Treasurer Robert R. Spencer
Bureau of Engineering
Wisconsin Department of Natural Resources
Box 450
Madison, Wisconsin 53701

7: YOUR CAREER IN FOREST FIRE MANAGEMENT

The threat of, and the damage done by, forest fires was a principal reason for the launching of the conservation movement in America. Gifford Pinchot's Forest Service was the organization that pioneered effective forest fire control, and the Forest Service is still the major agency in the country concerned with forest fires.

In the early days, fire was considered the greatest enemy of the woods and the most dangerous. For good reason. Devastating fires had been experienced wherever forest communities were established, logging was done, and piled-up slash acted as a fuse to set off what were literally explosions of fire when weather conditions were right. For example, a fire in Peshtigo, Wisconsin, in October 1871 destroyed the entire town of Peshtigo as well as some 2 million acres of magnificent white pine, and killed some 1,200 people. It was the worst natural disaster in the history of America.

It didn't take many experiences like Peshtigo to make people realize that fire was indeed a dangerous enemy in the woods. But there was no organization then in existence that could cope with the problem. Nor were there any men skilled in the science of forest fire fighting.

DEVELOPMENT OF ORGANIZED
FOREST FIRE CONTROL

Not until the Forest Service was created in 1905 did an organization exist that could begin taking effective action against forest fires. And it was not until 1910 that the Forest Service got its first real baptism of fire. That year one of the worst fires in America's history ran amuck in the forests of northern Idaho and western Montana. It burned several million acres of excellent timberland, destroyed much property, and took 187 lives. But for the first time, thanks to men of the Forest Service, effective work was done on fire lines, many lives were saved, and some towns that would surely have gone the way of Peshtigo were spared.

Costly though the year 1910 was, the Forest Service learned that year what was needed for effective organization to combat forest fires. It began building a fire combat organization that gained experience in subsequent years. It pioneered fire lookout towers on mountain peaks for earlier fire detection; telephone lines strung from the lookout to ranger and guard stations for faster communication; trails, roads, and bridges for faster transportation; and crew organization and methods for better fire fighting. The hard work and experience paid off. In 1934 conditions similar to those in 1910 existed in the northern Idaho forests. But in 1934, though fires did break out on the old Selway National Forest of Idaho, they were contained at 250,000 acres rather than 2 million, only 2 lives were lost rather than 187, and no great amount of property damage was suffered.

But even the 1934 fire was too costly. The Forest Service continued to develop the skills and techniques of forest fire control. It pioneered the use of aircraft to drop supplies to fire fighters in remote forest areas and the use of parachutists, known as smoke jumpers, for fast attack on fires. (The army adapted Forest Service methods in developing its own aerial drop and paratrooper techniques during World War II.) The Forest Service also pioneered aerial detection of fires by aircraft making regularly scheduled patrols of forested areas.

Average annual burned acreage on national forests greatly decreased. And in the meantime, other federal agencies as well as state and private forest organizations began adopting Forest Service methods and building their own effective forest fire control forces. Large forest fires still sometimes occur, particularly in California, an area highly susceptible to forest fire because of its long, hot, dry burning season and the presence of highly flammable brush fields. Bad fires continue to break out when conditions are right for them, just as bad floods develop when conditions are right, no matter how great the effort to prevent them.

But many potentially bad fires have been prevented, just as many bad floods have been prevented, by the precautionary work. For example, the Forest Service and other interested organizations, with the help of the National Advertising Council, made Smokey the Bear a household symbol, teaching the need to practice caution when dealing with fire in the woods. And when fires did start, expert fire control men quickly took action against them, and most of the fires were kept small.

For thirty years, from the 1930s to the 1960s, the annual amount of burned acreage continued to decrease because of the effective work of Forest Service and other fire control organizations. Millions of acres of fine timberland were saved that would surely have otherwise been destroyed by fire. Many lives were doubtless also saved, as was untold wealth in the form of property.

Then, in the 1960s the tide turned. Forest fires began to take a heavier annual toll of timbered acreage. This happened even though forest fire organizations had by then developed superb techniques and tools and recruited the best trained men possible to lead the attack against fire. What caused the reversal? Forest fire organizations had become too effective in combating the threat of fire in the woods.

FIRE MANAGEMENT VERSUS FIRE CONTROL

Today a leading forest fire fighter, William R. ("Bud") Moore, prefers to call his science forest fire management, rather than forest fire control. Bud Moore and I once worked on adjoining ranger districts as fire control men in Idaho. We were proud of our organizations and our ability to take action against a bust of fires, keeping them small by hitting them hard with all available men and tools. Our very effectiveness caused the increase in forest fires in the 1960s. On Moore's old district, along the North Fork of the Clearwater River in Idaho, lies one of the worst pile-ups of hazardous fuels in the country, and it has piled up primarily because Moore's organization has been so effective in keeping fire out of the country.

Bud Moore used his keen and questing mind to search out the truth about forest fire, its effects and its hazards. This led him to some startling conclusions. One is that fire can be a friend as well as an enemy in the woods.

Others besides Moore had come to this conclusion. The study of fire as an ecological tool rather than a complete enemy in the woods goes back many years. When he was still a young forester, Gifford Pinchot took note of the good effects fire can have in the forest. His favorite tree was the western larch, many magnificent specimens of which he found in western Montana, where fire has long played a dominant role in the ecological cycle because of dry summers and intense lightning storms. Pinchot admired the western larch because, as he wrote in a *National Geographic* article published in 1899, its "enormously thick bark is almost fireproof and so good a nonconductor that

Fire fighting crews battling a blaze. (*U.S. Forest Service*)

it protects the living tissue beneath it even against fires hot enough to scorch the trunk 50 or 75 feet above the ground." The western larch is a fire climax tree. *Because* of fire it is able to thrive in the western Montana forests. Fire destroys other growth that competes with the larch for available sunlight and moisture.

The same is true of a number of other valuable species of timber, including the magnificent sequoias of California. Pinchot pointed out in his 1899 article that these big trees "owe their power to reach an age of 3,000 or 4,000 years" to the fact that besides their great vitality, they are possessed of amazingly thick bark that protects them against ground fires.

Even earlier, John Muir, the California naturalist, took note of fire's role in the ecological cycle. Pinchot was aware of this.

In his 1899 article, he wrote: "A few observers who have lived much with the forest, such as John Muir of California, have grouped fire with temperature and moisture as one of the great factors which govern the distribution and character of forest growth."

In Muir's time, during the driest periods of summer, he could take a leisurely walk in the California forest surrounded by creeping ground fires and study them without hazard, because such regular burning kept the forest free of inflammatory brush and other ground fuels.

This is not to say that large, intense fires did not burn on the North American continent before European man set foot there. They did indeed, as the study of old, fire-scarred monarchs and the unearthing of charcoal remnants of ancient forests show. Some of these early large fires were probably touched off by Indians, who seem to have understood well the ecological role fire plays in the forest. Others were undoubtedly started by lightning, as is usually the case today. Insect epidemics that swept through forests and killed trees also contributed to the potential for big fires.

PRESCRIBED BURNING

We, like the Indians, can use fire as a tool in the forest by doing deliberately what nature does accidentally. This is known as prescribed burning.

The Indians, even the prehistoric Indians, used fire purposefully to create better game habitat. The aborigines of Australia did the same. In modern times prescribed burning goes back a number of years. H. H. Chapman, an outstanding pioneer American forester, as early as 1920 advocated deliberate burning to enhance longleaf pine propagation, and that has been done in the South for many years.

In heavily timbered northwestern America, Pinchot pointed to the Douglas fir as another fire-dependent species. "Here," he

An interagency fire center in Idaho. The dispatch office is the nerve center of activity for dispatching manpower, equipment, and supplies. (*U.S. Forest Service*)

wrote in 1899, "the young seedlings are found in remarkable abundance on unshaded spots wherever the vegetable covering of the mineral soil has been burned away." And he went on to note that "had fires been kept out of these forests in the last thousand years the fir which gives them their distinctive character would not be in existence, but would be replaced in all probability by the hemlock which fills even the densest of the Puget Sound forests with its innumerable seedlings." The hemlock is much inferior to the Douglas fir, which is today America's most valuable lumber tree.

Prescribed burning serves a most useful function in preparing a favorable seed bed for the favored species of timber, while lessening competition for sunlight and moisture.

But it is not just in connection with timber stand improvement that prescribed burning is done. State game departments are also beginning to use fire as a means of creating better game habitat.

Modern wildlife biologists note that where wildfire has swept, wildlife has thrived. The great fire that burned so much of northern Idaho in 1910 created forage for thousands of big game animals. Earlier, in the Clearwater country of Idaho, the Lewis and Clark party had found such dense forest and lack of game that they had to kill some of their horses to survive. The fire of 1910, and the later fire of 1934, created so much good game habitat that an elk herd of some 33,000 animals was established. Since then the elk have decreased in numbers, and hazardous fuels have built up, as a result of overzealous fire control. But along the Lochsa River, a tributary of the Clearwater, the Idaho State Game Department has been doing prescribed burning to re-create better big game habitat.

So successful has this program been, it is being expanded, with the Idaho Fish and Game Department and the Northern Region of the Forest Service cooperating in prescribed burning in the Spokane and Clearwater river drainages in the Coeur d'Alene, St. Joe, Clearwater, and Nezperce national forests. The purpose is to maintain the brushfield stage of plant succession to provide forage for Rocky Mountain elk, moose, mule deer and white-tailed deer and to sustain their populations within the productive capabilities of the land. The project proposals call for prescribed burning of 19,087 acres.

There is still another way fire works beneficially in the forest. The action of fire speeds up the return of minerals to the soil where they can be utilized by the young trees and other plants. The minerals are stored in the forest litter. Slowly they decompose and by leaching are returned to the soil. But that process takes years. Fire does the same thing quickly. It breaks down the complex organic molecules to smaller ones. When a fire changes a log to ash, nutrients bound in chemical compounds in the log are released and changed to a form that is water soluble. In this soluble form, nutrients percolating into the soil are again usable in the growth of other plants.

If, however, fire burns too intensely, not only can the soil be harmed, but some of the vital nutrients escape into the atmosphere, rather than being returned immediately to the soil. When a fire burns with great intensity, it leaves behind a wasteland. Many years must elapse before the sterile soil can again support plant life. And in the meantime, without plant life to guard the steep slopes, bad erosion results when pelting rain and snow runoff form rills and gulleys, and the valuable topsoil goes down to silt the streams and destroy aquatic life.

By prescribed burning, at the right time under the right conditions, man can control the fire's intensity but still allow its beneficial effects. This is a job that must be done by experts. Today fire management is a complex science.

WORKING IN FIRE MANAGEMENT

Good salaries are paid those who are expert in the new science of forest fire management, and because the work entails broad knowledge, along with leadership ability, forest fire managers can become leading administrators in general land management.

There is no particular college the interested student can attend to gain a degree in the science of forest fire management. The best advice is to take courses in forestry plus such other sciences as physics and chemistry. There is at least one excellent textbook available that can serve the student as a guide.

The book is *Forest Fires—Control and Use,* edited by Kenneth P. Davis, professor of forestry at Yale, and former president of the Society of American Foresters. Dr. Davis asked a number of persons in the forest fire control business to contribute to the book in their areas of expertise. The result is a compilation of the best material available on the subject, including ways of combating fire and ways of using it as an ecological tool.

Besides such study, the student should obtain summer employment in forest fire management with such agencies as the Forest Service, the Park Service, the Bureau of Land Management, and state forest organizations. Jobs are also available in private industry.

Forest fire management lends itself particularly well to part-time employment for students or for local residents of forested areas who are self-employed the rest of the year. Nevertheless, the Forest Service and other involved agencies do offer some full-time employment in fire management.

FIRE CONTROL AID

Fire control aids in the Forest Service receive on-the-job training and instruction in the maintenance of fire tools and equipment, as well as in safety methods and practices. When not performing fire control duties, they help maintain roads, trails, and other improvements, and work on brush disposal projects where they often participate in prescribed burning operations. Most fire control aids are paid at the GS-3 grade. After a year or so of experience they may advance to GS-4, and occasionally GS-5. The work generally runs from June to September, or during most school holidays, making it convenient for students.

FIRE LOOKOUT

Fire lookouts are assigned to lookout stations to detect and report fires, fire behavior, and other conditions related to fire occurrence and control, and to perform related fire control tasks. In filling these jobs, preference is often given to local residents familiar with topography, roads, and weather conditions. However, many college students are also placed on lookouts during the summer. Pay is at the GS-4 rate.

Fewer lookouts are hired now than in former times because aircraft is increasingly used for fire detection, but in many forests the stationary tower lookout is still considered essential for the best all-round system of fire detection. There are times when planes cannot fly, and these may be during periods when fire control is most critical. In my experience I have found that stationary lookouts often see hard-to-detect fires that aerial observers fail to note. In addition, they are essential as radio relay posts.

AERIAL OBSERVER

Aerial observer is a job that is open to students and other part-time employees of the Forest Service. The aerial observer, like the lookout, must have good eyesight and an expertise with maps so that he can quickly locate a fire accurately and report it to the nearest fire dispatcher. A pilot's license is not required, since this is strictly observation work.

Women can serve as well as men as aerial observers and lookouts. Often husband and wife teams are hired to staff lookouts.

Sally Fisher, Aerial Fire Observer

Sally Fisher was an aerial fire observer on the Nezperce National Forest in Idaho working seasonally during fire season. This large national forest is one of the worst fire forests in the country. As a result Sally gained lots of experience, and because of her good work was given another, similar assignment during the off-season. This was in connection with a tussock moth epidemic. The Forest Service found it necessary to conduct a spray program against the insect pest. Therefore, each morning at four thirty Sally boarded a small helicopter as an observer and then guided the spray helicopter following behind. Her duties included observing the spray cloud to see if local air currents caused it to drift uncontrollably, and warning the spray pilot of upcoming sensitive areas such as streams, springs, and ponds which had to be avoided to prevent possible contamination with the chemical spray.

DISPATCHER

Dispatchers, who man ranger district, forest, and regional headquarters, are skilled technicians with good background knowledge about forest fires, the techniques used in fighting them, and the country they are fought in. These persons have usually had some years of experience in fire control work. Theirs is a very responsible job, for they make the first move in dealing with a forest fire. They must make quick decisions, which often determine whether a fire is quickly controlled or gets out of hand.

The dispatcher must be a person who keeps cool and can work under intense pressure, speedily, but systematically. It is one of the fastest-thinking jobs in the world, for fire does not wait.

District dispatchers in the Forest Service are generally paid at the GS-7 grade, forest dispatchers at the GS-9 grade, and regional or zone dispatchers at GS-11 or higher. Most dispatchers are year-round employees who are given other duties during off-season.

FIRE CONTROL OFFICER

These men are skilled technicians with years of experience in forest fire control and general Forest Service field work. They used to be known as alternate rangers, for they often filled the

management, since this is proving such a useful ecological tool in maintaining our national parks. Fire management experts will also be needed in the various state game departments and in the Fish and Wildlife Service. There are some endangered species of wildlife, such as the Kirtland's warbler in Michigan, that cannot survive, just as certain valued species of timber cannot survive, unless fire continues to create the habitat they need.

Prescribed burning will become increasingly important on private as well as public timberlands to prepare adequate seed beds for the propagation of favored species of timber. Forest fire managers will be needed to supervise this work. They will play a major role in meeting our future timber needs.

Fire research will play an increasingly important role in forest fire management. The Forest Service maintains several multimillion-dollar fire research laboratories in different parts of the country. Here scientists work to gain new information on forest fire influences and effects. There are also fire control equipment development centers where new tools and techniques for fighting fires are worked out and tried. It was Forest Service fire control men who developed the first effective bulldozer more than forty years ago.

In short, there is a good future in forest fire management. The best way to get started is to apply for a part-time job with one of the public or private forestry organizations.

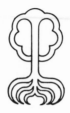

8: YOUR CAREER IN OUTDOOR RECREATION

Outdoor recreation is something most Americans take for granted. Ours is a big land, blessed with an abundance of natural resources that offers an infinite variety of outdoor recreational opportunities. Much of the land is still owned by all the people and is thus available to them to use for their pleasure as long as they do not violate certain rules and regulations set up for their protection as well as the protection of the resources they seek to enjoy. In reality, there are few restrictions. The land is there to be used, and it is being used with ever-increasing intensity. This last fact is why Americans should not take outdoor recreation for granted, and why a career in outdoor recreation is challenging. Outdoor recreation is a growth industry of almost unlimited potential.

THE NATIONAL PARK SERVICE

Since its inception in 1916 (though parks were in existence long before that) the National Park Service has been dedicated to the preservation and management of our country's scenic and historic areas. In 1964, the secretary of the interior recommended separate management concepts for three different types of areas —natural, historic, and recreational.

The national park system, which comprises almost 29 million acres, contains over 70 natural areas that preserve for future generations some of this country's natural beauty and grandeur; more than 165 historic areas that retell the story of the nation's growth; and over 30 recreational areas that provide space for physical recreation, relaxation, and restoration. The Park Service also administers the national capital parks in the Washington, D.C., metropolitan area. More than 6,000 employees form the permanent staff.

WORKING FOR THE PARK SERVICE

PARK RANGER

The best known and most popular job in the Park Service is that of park ranger. The service gets many more applications for the job than it can fill.

Park rangers perform a wide variety of professional duties related to the management of parks, historic sites, and recreation areas. The job category includes such former career designations as park historians, archeologists, and naturalists. The rangers' work includes planning and carrying out conservation efforts to protect plant and animal life in the parks from fire, disease, and heavy visitor usage. Rangers plan and conduct programs of public safety, including law enforcement and rescue work. They set up and direct interpretive programs such as slide shows, guided tours, displays, and dramatic presentations, all designed to help visitors become aware of the natural and historic significance of the area they are visiting.

Rangers work on recreation activity planning, conservation programs, park organization, financial management, supervision of other employees, and other activities related to the management of national park areas. They become involved in environmental educational programs and frequently take their message outside park boundaries. While on the job they are required to wear the prescribed uniform.

You may be surprised to learn that more than half of the rangers in the Park Service work in areas east of the Mississippi River. Though much work is performed outdoors, rangers often must work indoors in offices. This is especially true as they advance and assume more managerial responsibilities.

Most new rangers are hired at grade GS-7. Some new rangers are hired at grade GS-5. From the entry level, rangers move through the ranks to become subdistrict rangers, district rangers, park managers, and staff specialists in interpretation, resource management, park planning, and related areas.

Because of the ever-increasing number of "people" problems it must deal with, the Park Service looks for applicants who have an adequate grounding in the social and behavioral sciences. Ranger work is not primarily directed to research, and the Park Service does not seek out candidates with such backgrounds for ranger positions.

To qualify for park ranger positions at grade GS-5, you must have completed a full four-year course in an accredited college or university leading to a bachelor's degree with at least twenty-four semester hours in one or not more than two of the following: park and recreation management, any field-oriented natural science, history, archeology, political science, sociology, business administration, the behavioral sciences, or closely related subjects. Or you must have completed three years of park or conservation experience. In combining education with experience, an academic year of study (thirty semester hours or forty-five quarter hours) is considered equivalent to nine months' experience.

To qualify for grade GS-7 you must have one year of experience as a ranger or in work with similar responsibilities. One year of graduate study in appropriate courses can also qualify you. Another alternative is to meet the criteria for superior academic achievement.

To apply for a job as park ranger, take the federal service entrance examination. You can get information on this from the main post office in your area or from the nearest office of the U.S. Civil Service Commission. In addition to specifying one region of your choice, you should indicate in item 33 of the federal service entrance examination education and experience questionnaire that you wish to be considered in Washington, D.C.

If you are a college student, it is a good idea to inform the Park Service of your interest by writing to:

College Relations and Recruiting
National Park Service
Department of the Interior
18th and C Streets N.W.
Washington, D.C. 20240

Send a completed Standard Form 171 and a copy of your eligibility notice. Include a resume and a list of your college courses and grades. This may help you over some of the hurdles now existing in securing good employment with the Park Service.

Jerry Phillips, Park Ranger

Jerry Phillips, who grew up in the Denver area, decided early that he wanted to make a career with the Park Service. He loved the outdoors, and he loved visiting Rocky Mountain National Park in Colorado. Nothing could be better, he thought, than becoming a park ranger. But he knew he would have to prepare himself well for this. Therefore, he went to the University of Denver, and also the University of Colorado, majoring in such diverse subjects as architecture, European history, and plant morphology, and he received degrees in both history and botany. But while he was acquiring all this education, he managed to secure seasonal work in Rocky Mountain National Park, and that gave him the practical experience he needed. Upon graduation he secured a full-time appointment with the Park Service, and he became what is known today as a subdistrict ranger, the equivalent of assistant ranger, serving in Rocky Mountain National Park. That was in 1957.

Jerry Phillips served ten years at Rocky Mountain National Park, and while there was placed in charge of search and rescue, a job that calls for much hardiness and skill in the outdoors, since it often involves rescuing people in difficult circumstances—for example, stranded in inaccessible places where they have foolishly attempted to go, or lost in the wilds, or injured, or incapacitated.

In 1968 Jerry Phillips was promoted to the position of district ranger at Lake Mead in Arizona, one of the largest man-made lakes in the world, and where the Park Service manages a large recreation area. There are many law enforcement problems here, and Ranger Phillips gained much experience in this type of activity—so much that he became a recognized expert. In 1972 he was transferred to Yellowstone, first and largest of all the national parks, and placed in charge of law enforcement.

When I visited Jerry in Yellowstone in August 1974, he was serving as chief ranger of Yellowstone while the regular chief park ranger, Harold J. Estey, was out of the park on business. I asked Jerry what advice he could give others who might want to emulate him.

"Education is important," he emphasized, and proceeded to tell of his own educational background. I remarked on the diversity of his education.

"I've found that to be useful too," he said. "Learning about plants was practical, but history is important too, as is architecture. You have use for all these things in the Park Service, and a lot more too."

"But what about law enforcement?" I asked him. "How in the world did you ever come to specialize in that?"

"Well," he said with a chuckle, "I suppose that was a matter of necessity. All rangers have to deal with it. We deal with all kinds of people, most of whom are very fine folks. But because we have to deal with so many people, it's very important for those who want to become park rangers to study the social sciences. I can't emphasize that enough."

PARK AIDS AND TECHNICIANS

In years past most of the work—aside from maintenance—in the national parks was done by rangers and other professionals. But increasingly aids and technicians are taking over duties once considered the prerogative of full-time professionals. To become an aid or technician in the Park Service, you do not need a college degree.

A job as park aid is the first step to a career as park technician. Through on-the-job experience park aids develop their skills and knowledge of practical park operations. Aids work at the more basic tasks involved in fire fighting, conservation programs, providing information to the public, enforcing the law, operating campgrounds, and other jobs related to park and recreation area operations.

Technicians perform a wide variety of functions, usually following the direction or plans of park rangers. In historic and archeological areas technicians carry out plans to preserve and restore buildings and sites. They operate campgrounds, assigning sites, replenishing firewood, performing safety inspections, and providing information to visitors.

Technicians lead guided tours and give talks to groups of visitors. They operate projectors and sound equipment for slide shows and movies. Technicians direct traffic, go on road patrols, operate radio dispatch stations, and perform other law enforcement and public safety functions.

Park aids usually start at GS-2 or GS-3. Park technicians can start at grade GS-4 and advance as high as GS-9. All applicants must submit their qualifications to the U.S. Civil Service Commission for review and rating. Applicants for park aid jobs must pass a written civil service test.

To qualify as a park aid you generally must have six months

to one year of experience in a park or similar situation. You may also qualify if you have finished high school and, for GS-3 positions, have completed one year of college level studies.

To qualify as a park technician, you generally need at least two years' experience in a park or similar situation or two years of college level studies relating to park operations. Attending one of the two-year vocational schools listed in appendix A can be a big asset.

You can begin applying for a nonprofessional Park Service job by contacting the nearest office of the U.S. Civil Service Commission. You can also obtain information from the main post office in your area. For a park aid job, the Civil Service Commission will tell you the name of the written test to take in your area of the country. For a park technician job at grade GS-4, ask to be rated under the technical assistant examination. There is no written test, just a review of your experience and education.

If there is a particular Park Service area you would like to work in, you may write the park superintendent and inform him of your interest. Include an extra copy of your application and notice of rating. If you possibly can, visit in person. There is no substitute for a personal interview to prove your desire and sincerity and to sell your personality.

PARK GUIDES

Park guides give talks, answer questions, conduct groups of visitors in or through an area, and supply general information concerning the area or facility and its features. These positions may be temporary or permanent. Entry level is usually at grade GS-4. The junior federal assistant examination is the required test for these positions. An applicant must pass the written examination and meet the experience requirements outlined in the announcement. You may request information from the National Park Service regional office that has jurisdiction over the geographical area in which you seek employment.

Marinas create job opportunities.

PARK GUARDS

Guards are hired to protect property and buildings. The usual entry level is GS-3. Parks fill these positions locally from lists of eligibles established by Civil Service Commission interagency boards. You may request information from the National Park Service regional office that has jurisdiction over the geographical area in which you seek employment. Generally, competition in guard examinations is limited to those persons entitled to veterans' preference.

SEASONAL JOBS

There is opportunity for seasonable employment in the national parks, though the competition for these jobs is keen. A large majority of the positions are filled each year by men and women who have worked for the service one or more seasons.

Initial grade level for seasonal positions ranges from GS-2 to GS-4. All seasonal rangers and many seasonal technicians and aids are required to wear the official National Park Service uniform, which must be purchased by the appointee prior to his first day on duty. An initial allowance of up to $125 is paid to seasonal employees for this purpose. Because many seasonal positions require individuals in excellent physical condition, a medical examination may be needed, at your own expense, before appointment.

The Park Service also hires student assistants for seasonal work.

Seasonal lifeguards are hired for lifesaving and rescue work. The best job opportunities are at Assateague Island, Cape Cod, Cape Hatteras, Fire Island, Lake Mead, Padre Island, and Point Reyes. Qualifications include lifeguard eligibility in the summer employment examination conducted by the Civil Service Commission. Persons seeking positions at ocean beaches must successfully complete an on-site, surf-rescue training course.

Your application for seasonal employment must be received by the National Park Service between January 1 and February 15. Many parks accept applications only until they have a sufficient number to take care of their needs; in many cases, this may be as early as January 15. Therefore, apply as soon after January 1 as possible. If you are applying for a position that requires you to pass the summer employment examination, apply for the test between November and early February.

EMPLOYMENT OPPORTUNITIES OUTSIDE THE PARK SERVICE

THE FISH AND WILDLIFE SERVICE

The Fish and Wildlife Service has in recent years greatly increased its outdoor recreation projects.

The recreation program on the national wildlife refuges can

be somewhat special, since most visitors go to the refuges to view the wildlife. But increasingly, they are finding more varied recreational opportunities on the refuges, including hunting, fishing, swimming, boating, hiking, and photography.

Most refuges are large enough to accommodate many visitors without unduly disturbing the birds and animals they were established to protect. Yearly recreation visits approach the 25 million mark. Over 330 refuges totaling 30 million acres were in the system as of 1971.

About 180 national wildlife refuges have resident staffs. These employees also may be responsible for the management of nearby unstaffed refuges. Increasingly, recreation specialists are being hired as part of the staff of the most popular refuges.

During 1970, the refuge system experimented in a new phase of the public use program. Three students in the recreation and parks administration curriculum of Pennsylvania State University carried out their ten-week work experience (practicum) at Chincoteague Refuge, Virginia, and Crab Orchard Refuge, Illinois. These refuges provided the physical base and staff supervision that enabled the students to complete requirements for the bachelor of science degree. All the participants proved extremely able in planning and programing various refuge public use operations. Since the pilot phase of the student practicum proved successful, it is now planned to extend the program to other schools with similar curriculum requirements. Your school could be one of these. Very likely other agencies will be competing more and more for students in these valuable practicum programs.

Recent years have seen a distinct rise in vandalism, theft, assault, and other crimes in outdoor recreation areas, and national wildlife refuges are no exception. This calls for increased protection by patrols and other means, and outdoor recreation protection can become a career in itself, as it did for Jerry Phillips of the Park Service.

The 187 million acres of the national forests and the national grasslands have been described as the world's largest outdoor playground. They contain more than 7,000 camp and picnic grounds, by far the largest number on any kind of land, public or private. They have the most winter sports areas, 200 of them, financed privately and operated under paid permits, capable of accommodating over 300,000 persons at a time. In addition, the national forests have many other types of recreation facilities— swimming beaches, boat launching ramps, hiking trails, interpretive centers. And they contain by far the greatest amount of proclaimed wilderness in the national wilderness system.

Recreation Workers

Every ranger district has employees whose primary duties lie in recreation management. Many are seasonal employees, hired as recreation aids or technicians at levels ranging from GS-2 to GS-9. National forests have recreation staff officers, usually rating GS-12, and regional offices have quite large recreational staffs, with positions ranging from about GS-11 to GS-15. The Washington office also has a large recreational staff, with the chief of the recreation division rating a GS-16 grade.

Snow Ranger, Ski Patrolman

Because the national forests are so popular for outdoor winter sports, particularly skiing and snowmobiling, the job of snow ranger has come into existence to counter the threat of the killer avalanche in the western mountains.

As for so many other outdoor jobs in the Forest Service, a man must be in excellent physical condition to be a snow ranger. Besides that, he must be an expert skier and an accomplished mountaineer. He must like to work with people (im-

Increased wilderness use means more wilderness management jobs.

portant in all outdoor recreation jobs), should have at least a high school education and an understanding of such subjects as geology, physics, and other natural sciences. He must know about snow, terrain, wind, and weather. This will help him to forecast avalanches and guard against them. He may also be called upon to trigger off avalanches, by using artillery or blasting with dynamite. He'll put up hazard signs. His principal duty is to protect the public from the hazards of deep snow on steep mountain slopes. It takes an exceptional man to do this, and he must be well trained. The Forest Service now sponsors an annual avalanche training school for this purpose, and it attracts snow recreation people from across the nation as well as from countries as far away as Japan.

Ski patrolmen, and the ski patrols they organize, are primarily charged with rescue work, warning of dangerous conditions, and the elimination of hazards, such as the threat of avalanches. The ski patrol leader and at least two members of each patrol have to meet the national ski patrol system standard requirements for first-aid training and for skiing ability.

Ski patrolmen and snow rangers are in increasing demand because of the rise in snowmobiling on the national forests and other public lands. These machines can break down, stranding their riders in rugged, isolated winter terrain. Accidents can happen that seriously injure the riders. Rescues must then be made and often first aid given to the injured.

Wilderness Ranger

The increased use of wilderness by backpackers and horseback riders has brought about the need for the recreation specialist known as the wilderness ranger, whose primary duty is wilderness and backcountry management. He too must be a rugged person, and possess a deep love for the wilderness.

THE TENNESSEE VALLEY AUTHORITY

The TVA promotes outdoor recreation to demonstrate how it can be utilized as a resource for economic development of an area.

In Kentucky and Tennessee the TVA is developing Land Between The Lakes. The project involves a 170,000-acre isthmus in western Kentucky and Tennessee between two of the largest man-made lakes in the nation. On this land the TVA is creating a major outdoor recreation and conservation education area to show how terrain with limited forestry, agricultural, and mineral resources can be developed as a recreation asset that will serve the American people and at the same time bolster the economy of the surrounding region.

This new development will have facilities to serve millions of users with the widest range of outdoor recreation and education interests. Visitors will be able to camp, fish, swim, boat, hike, picnic, and study their natural surroundings. The area's 300

miles of shoreline, rolling hills, and fields and forests will make
Land Between The Lakes attractive to all who seek rest, relaxation, and recreation. Eventually, an estimated 10 million Americans will use the facilities annually.

The Recreation Services Section hires recreation planners,
recreation area assistants, and park attendants. Pay scales range
from around $3 an hours to as much as $16,735 a year.

The TVA also has an interesting program for college students in practicum recreation programs. College students from
eleven midwestern and southern universities and colleges provide supervised recreational programs during the summer for
thousands of visitors to Land Between The Lakes. Other students assist in workshop training programs for teachers and
students within the 5,000-acre Environmental Education Center.
Interns assist in the information section, working on new trail
systems, doing historical research, and running tests on the water
supply and sewage treatment plants.

Bob Howes and Land Between The Lakes

Robert M. Howes began working for the TVA soon after
the organization came into existence. In 1933 he had gained
a bachelor of science degree from Massachusetts State College (now the University of Massachusetts at Amherst) with
a major in landscape architecture. He also edited the *Index,*
the college yearbook, and worked as college correspondent
for *The Springfield Republican,* a newspaper. Learning to
use words in this manner was important for him in the
career he chose.

In 1934 Bob Howes gained a bachelor of landscape architecture degree from the University of Massachusetts, continuing his job as newspaper correspondent and doing graduate work in landscape forestry, resource administration,
ecology, recreation, and English. He could scarcely have
prepared himself better for his career.

He went to work for the TVA on June 1, 1934, at what was
then the good annual salary of $1,296. He began work in
Knoxville, Tennessee, as junior landscape draftsman in the

Outdoor recreation specialists care for people's needs and enforce the rules and regulations governing camping and other recreation areas.

Division of Land Planning and Housing. For six months he served a period of indoctrination for later work in regional development of park and recreation resources.

During the next several years Bob Howes was assigned various types of jobs, many of which involved working in the field and all of which broadened his experience. He became an authority on recreation in the valley. His pay gradually increased until by 1938 he was making $3,200 a year, again a decent salary for those times.

Beginning in 1938, Howes was given even broader responsibility. The TVA was now studying recreation resources resulting from development of its system of multipurpose reservoirs. Howes was assigned to prepare reports on a number of individual reservoirs and, in 1939, a review of the entire system.

Early during World War II Howes was involved in community planning for war-related impacts. Then he served as a line officer in the navy, primarily in the Pacific theater.

In 1946 he resumed his career with the TVA. For the next eight years he served as chief of the recreation relations staff. Recreation was becoming increasingly important in the Tennessee Valley, as everywhere else, and the TVA had much to offer recreation enthusiasts. The organization had greatly enhanced recreation opportunities in the region through its creation of huge, multipurpose reservoirs, as well as its effective restoration of lands and forests.

In 1954 Howes's work was expanded to include all forms of reservoir shoreline use, including forest, agricultural, industrial, residential, and utility use as well as recreation. He advanced in classification to chief of the Property Use Section and to assistant director of reservoir properties. In 1959 he was designated the TVA's representative on the Advisory Council to the Outdoor Recreation Resources Review Commission whose report, *Outdoor Recreation for America*, was published in 1962. By this time, Bob Howes was making $14,600 per year.

In 1960 Howes became director of reservoir properties, one of the most important jobs in the TVA. His responsibilities included administration, policy forming, and related duties concerning management of public land and land rights in TVA custody along 10,000 miles of reservoir shoreline in seven states.

As director of reservoir properties, Howes proposed the Land Between The Lakes, which he envisioned as a national demonstration in the development of underutilized land and water resources for public outdoor recreation and environmental education. The proposal soon gained enthusiastic support, including that of President John F. Kennedy, who made the TVA responsible for implementing the idea. Bob Howes was the logical choice for first director of Land Between The Lakes, a position he held until his retirement in September 1974.

Howes, still living in the TVA region, has the leisure now to enjoy some of the same recreational opportunities he brought to so many others. It is hard to imagine a more useful and satisfying career in the outdoors or anywhere else.

Over the past thirty years the recreation program at Army Corps of Engineers lakes and waterways has grown from an incidental amenity to a major project providing outdoor recreation opportunities for millions of Americans. In just twenty years attendance at corps lakes and waterways has grown seventeenfold (to more than 250 million), while the number of water resource projects has increased only eightfold. For a number of years the corps has recorded the largest outdoor recreation attendance of any single agency. Today recreation is considered a major purpose in calculating costs and benefits of a potential project.

The corps manages over 10 million acres of land and water across the nation. Its policy is to encourage and accommodate sustained public use of the recreation resource, up to the maximum carrying capacity consistent with ecological, aesthetic, and historical values. This is called recreation resource management.

Recreation resource management requires a knowledge of basic conservation policies, an appreciation of recreation use as an important project function, and foresight in planning to meet the increasing demands for water-oriented recreation. Its aim is to manage all resources, both developed and natural, as an integrated whole, avoiding or minimizing the conflict among different types of uses.

The corps manages some 390 lakes and waterways projects. Some 2,450 developed recreational areas, including approximately 1,500 day use and 950 overnight use areas, are available for public enjoyment at corps projects. The corps must hire a great many recreation specialists and workers to develop and maintain these facilities. It compares with and competes with other government agencies in pay scales for these employees, and constantly recruits them. Basically the corps seeks a combination of skills and interests enabling people to view lands and waters, fish and wildlife, forest and vegetative cover, and other elements of the ecosystem as interrelated and relevant functions of the entire resources program.

Some states in recent years have made great strides in upgrading their outdoor recreation potential. Illinois is a good example. There a greater emphasis is being given to preserving the state's natural areas and areas of historical importance. Illinois has hired many people with requisite skills and dedication to do the job of historical and natural preservation.

States and their political subdivisions have become the major suppliers of most forms of outdoor recreation opportunity. Comprehensive statewide recreation plans have been developed by all fifty states. Since 1965, state and local governments have added a total of approximately 1.5 million acres to their park systems and public recreation areas, bringing the number of acres in such systems to 36.5 million in the fifty states. There are five times as many visits to areas administered by state and local governments as to areas administered by agencies of the federal government. Hence, there are many more recreation job opportunities in the individual states. The popular Illinois Beach State Park, near Chicago, has as many as 250,000 visitors on a holiday weekend, such as the Fourth of July. State parks are close to our largest urban areas. A large number of employees and much careful planning are needed to maintain the high quality of these areas under such intensive use. A lot of money is needed, too.

The land and water conservation fund was created in 1965 to provide federal grants to states for recreation and to finance various federal recreation programs. In 1968, Congress amended the enabling act to provide that revenues from outer continental shelf mineral leasing programs (offshore oil drilling primarily) could be used to guarantee an annual level of $200 million to the fund. This provision ended in 1973. The Nixon administration impounded moneys meant for the fund just when it was beginning to hit its stride. But the act is still on the books, the needs are clearly recognized, and when the fund is again fully activated (as it must be if we are to meet our outdoor recreation needs), many more jobs will be made available in outdoor recreation management.

THE PRIVATE SECTOR

One of the good effects of the development of public outdoor recreational opportunities is the concurrent development of privately owned recreational facilities. This in turn creates many recreational job opportunities in the private sector.

For example, each time the Army Corps of Engineers creates a large impoundment of water, many new businesses develop that cater to recreationists. To date, concessionaires, as well as other public agencies, have about matched corps funds expended for development, operation, and maintenance of recreation facilities at corps projects.

The same thing has happened in the Tennessee Valley. The TVA lakes and shorelines continue to be the focal point for much of the outdoor recreation in the region. Private citizens, commercial enterprises, and public agencies invested more than $40 million in recreation facilities and improvements on and around the lakes during 1971 alone. That brought the total recreation investment to more than $350 million, an increase of more than $200 million in the past decade. The figures do not include developments in the TVA's Land Between The Lakes recreation area.

Many of the large marinas and resorts need people who are skilled in outdoor sports, who can guide hunting and fishing parties, who have the mechanical skills to keep equipment in top shape, and who otherwise know how to cater to outdoor recreationists.

To get a job like this, the first requirement is to learn how to get along with a variety of people, some of them highly skilled in the outdoor arts, others rank greenhorns. You must know how to treat people differently, but always courteously and well. Because many will rely on you for the skills they lack, you must yourself become proficient in such outdoor skills as boating, camping, hunting, and fishing. You should also have mechanical ability. You don't have to be an expert all at once, however. Attitude and aptitude are most important. If you have these in sufficient quantity, you can learn the requisite degree of skill.

The best way to get such a job is to apply in person. Get acquainted with your local resort owners. Let them know of your interest. Chances are good one of them will give you at least part-time work to start with, and a full-time job as you gain experience. Eventually you may even decide to go into business for yourself.

Bob Karbowski, Resort Manager

A good example is Bob Karbowski, who runs the popular Four Seasons Resort on Lake Winnibigoshish in northern Minnesota. Big Winnie, as the lake is called, was created partially by an Army Corps of Engineers project and it is surrounded by Chippewa National Forest. Bob, a rugged outdoorsman and skilled hunter and fisherman, made his resort one of the best on the big lake and employs as many as a dozen people to help him run it, a number of them local Chippewa Indians. He is in business year round, catering to snowmobilers and ice fishermen in winter, and to fishermen and outdoor enthusiasts during the summer. He has his own cabins to rent, his own private boat dock, and boats, snowmobiles and other types of sports equipment to rent. He runs a good restaurant besides. It takes a number of skilled people to help him run his business successfully.

EDUCATIONAL OPPORTUNITIES

According to the National Science Foundation's Commission on Education in Agriculture and Natural Resources, twenty of the fifty land-grant colleges and several universities that teach courses in agriculture offer options and curricula in outdoor recreation and park management.

A majority of the forty forestry schools offer options in forestry recreation and/or park management. These options are in addition to the standard curricula and major areas of study already provided by the schools of agriculture and forestry to prepare students for careers in the natural resource management area.

Many of the technical schools listed in Appendix A also offer good outdoor recreation courses. Write for catalogs from the schools nearest you, and see what they have to offer. Keep in mind the wide variety of skills needed in outdoor recreation jobs. Learn one or more of these skills well, by attending one of these schools, and you will see your opportunities greatly increased.

FUTURE PROSPECTS

The wild and scenic rivers program started out with eight rivers in America placed in the National Wild and Scenic Rivers System to preserve their best qualities and offer the American people outdoor recreational opportunities. Twenty-seven more rivers are being considered for addition to the system. Each one will create additional opportunities for outdoor recreation, which in turn will create many new recreational jobs.

There is a growing public awareness for the need to preserve our outdoor heritage for the enjoyment of our own and future generations. Many skilled and dedicated people will be needed to do the job.

For more information contact:

Izaak Walton League of America
1800 North Kent Street, Suite 806
Arlington, Virginia 22209

The National Conference on State Parks
1601 North Kent Street, Suite 1100
Arlington, Virginia 22209

National Parks and Conservation Association
1701 18th Street N.W.
Washington, D.C. 20009

National Recreation and Park Association
1601 North Kent Street
Arlington, Virginia 22209

National Wildlife Federation
1412 16th Street N.W.
Washington, D.C. 20036

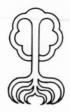

9: YOUR CAREER IN OUTDOOR INFORMATION AND EDUCATION

Gifford Pinchot, the man who organized and led the conservation crusade in America, preached that nothing is more important in a democratic country like America than informing the people so that they understand the basic tenets of conservation and support those who seek to carry out those tenets in managing the public's natural resouces.

Pinchot was not alone in this observation. All the great leaders in conservation realized the importance of information and education in gaining their goals. Many wrote articles and books about it, and gave lectures. They sought in every way they could to inform and educate the people, for they knew that without the people's support their cause was hopeless.

When he first took over the old Division of Forestry in the U.S. Department of Agriculture, Pinchot was amazed at how little was done in the area of informing the public. He began immediately to change that. In September 1899 he published the first volume of *Primer of Forestry*. It was distributed by his division and by the U.S. Senate, and eventually had a circulation of 1.3 million copies. Pinchot followed with other informative booklets and pamphlets.

In *Breaking New Ground* he wrote:

> *Far more important, however, than any publication was the good understanding the Division was establishing with the newspapers. They printed hundreds of millions of copies in a year, and their items about our work reached a thousand readers to our bulletins' one. Forestry was beginning to be news.*

Today, of course, Pinchot would include the electronic news media along with newspapers. Radio and television news combined reaches more people than do newspapers themselves. Still, newspapers remain important information sources and are carefully read by so-called decision makers and other key people in our society.

THE WORK OF INFORMING AND EDUCATING

An important part of the information and education (I&E) job is working with the news media. Certain skills and techniques are involved in this, and not everyone is well equipped to develop them. Effective I&E calls for well-motivated people with requisite aptitudes and skills.

The better conservation organizations know that people trained in the relevant scientific disciplines are not always the best ones to head up a public information section. One of the most effective I&E men I ever worked with was the late Clint Davis, who for many years directed public information for the Forest Service, and who helped make Smokey the Bear a household symbol. Clint was not a forester. He was a trained newspaperman, developer of one of the earliest outdoor columns for the Atlanta *Constitution*. He had the greatest technique for working with news media people that I have ever seen. He spoke their language, understood their problems, and gave them what they needed to do a good job of reporting.

It's interesting that Gifford Pinchot, soon after the Forest Service was founded, hired the editor of a small newspaper in Hamilton, Montana, as one of his principal assistants. Pinchot didn't hire the editor for his knowledge about the new science of forestry; he hired him for his ability to communicate with people.

I do not mean that foresters and biologists cannot be good I&E people. Some have been outstanding. If you are now studying a discipline such as forestry or biology and also have a strong urge to get into I&E work, don't hesitate to do so. When you can combine basic scientific knowledge with I&E skills, you have a combination that is hard to beat and one that will open up many career opportunities for you.

Information is half the job in I&E. The other half is education. The two are closely related, but there are some differences. A good information specialist is not necessarily a good education specialist. And vice versa. But the people who combine the two talents are the best in the business.

Educators in the conservation agencies must have the same skills and use many of the same techniques required for regular teaching jobs in the schools. Many of them come to the agencies from schoolroom teaching and they carry the agency's message to the schools. In a sense they are propagandizers, for they are selling their agencies to the schools, but as educators they must be sure to have their facts straight and to present them honestly.

Educators, if they are to be most effective, must carry their message to other places besides the schools. They too utilize newspapers and other news media. Many of these have education editors or writers and environment editors or writers. The agency educators work through these newsmen to reach many thousands of readers and viewers. They also work with labor group leaders, civic and women's groups, and the like. People

Designing exhibits for visitor centers is an important information and education job.

in all walks of life are concerned about the environment and ecology and are eager to learn about these vital subjects.

This eagerness to learn has brought about a new discipline in information and education work, one that is closely related to outdoor recreation. This is the science of interpretation. Many conservation agencies hire people skilled in this science. It involves the interpretation of plants and animals and natural phenomena to give laymen a better understanding and appreciation of them. Practitioners of this science are often called interpretive naturalists.

Information and education in conservation is today a broad activity. Essentially its mission is to inform and educate the people about the work and the problems of the agencies.

Pinchot and other early conservationists preached that the

agencies must not only do a good job of conserving natural resources, but must tell the people they are doing a good job so they can continue to have the people's support. I would add that they must *prove* to the people they are doing a good job. And this requires special skills and techniques.

WRITING AND THE VISUAL ARTS

Just as information and education combine to prove that an agency is doing a good job of natural resources conservation, so do writing and photography combine to communicate the message. And those of us who possess skill in one—or better both— are much in demand for I&E work.

Many people attracted to I&E work can learn writing techniques as well as photographic techniques. But to be a skilled writer, you need to have a strong aptitude for the craft and a love for words. Writing can be a real chore for those who do not. I have known many agency people who have hated writing more than any other part of their activities. Though they may be good in other areas, those people are generally not good in I&E.

Aptitude is the key word. If you want to be a writer you usually know it. You love words and you love to use them.

Aptitude in the visual arts, including photography, is also important. Some say the visual arts will eventually supplant the written word. I think there will always be a need for both, but the visual arts are undeniably effective in informing and educating the public about natural resource conservation.

Skilled layout people are in demand in information and education divisions involved in publishing, as most of them are today. Often photography, artwork, and layout skills go hand in hand. That more than makes up for such an individual's lack of writing skill. Therefore, those who want to get into I&E work, and who know they can never qualify as accomplished writers,

An interpretive naturalist explains the stalagmites and stalactites in the Lewis and Clark Cavern in Montana.

Nature interpretation is an important part of this TVA education specialist's job.

need not despair. Artistic ability will more than compensate for lack of writing ability. Mastery of photographic and layout skills can assure a good career in I&E work.

I&E work is increasingly well paid. A good writer in the government can command a salary of $20,000 a year, and good artists and photographers, after they become established, can do as well.

WORKING FOR GOVERNMENT AGENCIES

I&E work dovetails with just about all the other kinds of jobs described in this book. The careers of Bill Colpitts, John

Forssen, and Paul Steucke illustrate the opportunities available in I&E work.

Bill Colpitts, I&E Combined with Recreation Work

I first became acquainted with William L. Colpitts when I served as press officer for the Eastern Region of the Forest Service, with headquarters in Milwaukee. Bill's office adjoined mine. We were both staff officers in the information and education division of this important Forest Service region that covers twenty states from Maine to Minnesota to Missouri to Maryland, and contains in all seventeen national forests. Over half the country's population resides in this one region. Hence there is a tremendous amount of I&E work, and recreation use on these national forests is also heavy.

Bill Colpitts, as regional officer in charge of interpretive services and conservation education from 1961 to 1967, was instrumental in planning and developing three major visitor centers on the national forests, as well as many interpretive nature trails. He was called upon often by other groups as a consultant and expert in outdoor education and nature interpretation.

Bill was raised in southern Indiana. He thought nothing could be better than to make his living working outdoors. But he knew he would need to educate himself well to succeed. Therefore he entered Indiana University and in 1956 secured a degree in outdoor recreation and park management, with minors in biological science and elementary education. While getting his formal education, he worked three summer seasons as a park naturalist in the Indiana state parks.

Upon completion of academic work (he spent another year in graduate study) Bill secured appointment as educational adviser for the Indiana Department of Conservation in 1957. For four and a half years in this position he conducted classes, workshops, and training courses. He also formed the Indiana Conservation Education Advisory Committee, which developed a state curriculum guide. And he wrote monthly articles for the state publication, *Outdoor Indiana*.

His competent work in Indiana enabled Bill to secure an

appointment with the U.S. Forest Service. In 1967 he was promoted to the Washington, D.C., headquarters of the service, where he served three years as section chief for visitor services in the Division of Information and Education. From there he was recruited by the U.S. Fish and Wildlife Service to head up its branch of public use for all the national wildlife refuges. Then in 1974 he was recruited for still another type of job in another type of agency. He became chief of park services for all the parks in Montgomery County, Maryland. Montgomery County, which adjoins the nation's capital, has a population of approximately 600,000 and a larger system of parks than many states have. There are nearly 300 parks with 18,273 acres, and since 1973 they have been serving over 9 million persons annually. The outdoor education and conservation programs in the Montgomery County parks, for children as well as adults, are probably some of the best in the country.

John Forssen, Writer

John Forssen followed a different road to a career in I&E. He studied journalism in his native New Hampshire, and after graduation went to work for a small newspaper. Soon he secured another job as an editor on a magazine published in Wisconsin. I first became acquainted with him when he was interviewed for the job of writer-editor for the Eastern Region of the Forest Service. Though John was quite young and lacked a background in forestry or other matters relating to the Forest Service, his writing ability was impressive. The Forest Service background could be taught him.

John's main duties were writing news releases, brochures, special and annual reports, and occasional feature articles. Besides writing ability, he had artistic talent. He helped illustrate many of the things he wrote. And he had a quick mind that soon grasped the fundamentals of the organization he was working for. Moreover, he had in the regional office some of the best experts in the world on the outdoor subjects he needed to write about.

One of John's annual reports won first prize in a national contest for such government reports. He also received a meritorious award for his fine work. He stayed with the Forest Service for about five years, gaining excellent background experience. Then he accepted a position as teacher of creative writing at Pennsylvania State University—a post from which he can influence many young writers to embrace the outdoor field and write well about it.

Paul Steucke, Artist-Photographer

Paul Steucke was raised in the Washington, D.C., area where his father was a government official. Paul had natural artistic talent and put himself through art school. He was able to utilize his schooling and his talent when he came to work for the Forest Service in the Eastern Region headquarters, heading up the Audio-Visual Section in the Division of Information and Education. In this job Paul was responsible for all the graphic arts, including layout work for publications. He was also in charge of mechanical reproduction equipment, such as movie and still cameras, tape recorders, and the like. He had mastered photography along with his other talents.

Paul Steucke spent a good deal of time on the various national forests in the Eastern Region, and the photographic file in the Milwaukee headquarters shows the results of his fine work. But besides that, Paul and his assistants put out some of the most beautiful pamphlets and brochures that any government agency has ever published.

He was soon promoted to the Washington, D.C., headquarters of the Forest Service, where for a time he held a key job in graphic arts for the Division of Information and Education. But Paul was more than just a talented artist and skilled photographer. He had learned much about general I&E work, and when an opportunity came to take a key job with the Water Resources Council, he accepted. Paul is today a respected official of an important government conservation agency in his own home area, able to put his talents to good use in informing the people about our most important water resources.

WORKING IN THE PRIVATE SECTOR

Many private conservation organizations hire information and education experts to help them get their particular message out to the people. Many produce their own magazines and other publications and thus have need for skilled writers, photographers, and editors.

The forest products industries, for example, hire many writers and editors for industry publications—news releases, newsletters, special feature articles, radio and television scripts, annual reports, advertisements, displays and exhibits, sales literature, brochures, and speeches.

Numerous industry associations also hire I&E specialists whose job is to communicate with the executives of member companies to keep them informed of new developments and brief them on upcoming or current legislation affecting the industry. Specialists in government affairs present information to congressmen to keep them informed on timber growing, manufacturing, and consumer issues.

These are well-paid jobs, some of them very well paid. In most cases they require a college degree, often an advanced degree.

FUTURE PROSPECTS

Public agencies have had to reduce their I&E staffs in recent years because of manpower and budget restrictions. But the need for these specialists continues to grow, there are many jobs to fill, and the agencies will be recruiting increasing numbers of qualified people.

Past ecological mismanagement coupled with the rapid rise of technology and the consequent industrialization and urbanization could render much of our environment unfit for existence unless certain of our habits are drastically changed. To accomplish this, a mammoth educational effort must be mounted, directed at both youth and adults. New learning programs will be needed for the schools. Supporting agencies having environmental goals in common with the schools must assist them to achieve their goals. Children will have to be taken out of the classrooms more and more so that they can learn environmental facts at first hand in areas established for that purpose.

EEE stands for environmental-ecological education. There are more than a hundred colleges involved in EEE studies. They are needed, for, according to *Changing Times,* the Kiplinger magazine, "the 'national shortage' of professionals in the environment-related fields doesn't appear likely to diminish."

There is the challenge. Get yourself a good education, enter this field, and know that you are embarked not only on a most useful career, but on one that should compensate you in many ways.

For more information contact:

Association for Environmental and Outdoor Education
2428 Walnut Boulevard
Walnut Creek, California 94596

Association of Interpretive Naturalists
6700 Needwood Road
Derwood, Maryland 20855

Conservation Education Association
c/o Secretary Treasurer Robert O. Ellingson
Department of Natural Resources
Box 450
Madison, Wisconsin, 53701

National Association for Environmental Education
1011 S.W. 140 Street
Miami, Florida 33156

Outdoor Writers Association of America, Inc.
4141 West Bradley Road
Milwaukee, Wisconsin 53209

Western Regional Environmental Education Council
721 Capitol Mall
Sacramento, California 95814

Appendix A

TECHNICAL SCHOOLS AND COLLEGES

So many schools and colleges offer courses for oudoor technicians that it is difficult to list them all. The advantage is the student's, since no matter where he lives, he will not have to travel far to find instruction.

I have personally investigated some of these schools and have relied on others, whose opinion I respect, to advise on some. That and the recommendation of such organizations as the U.S. Forest Service, the American Forest Institute, and the Wisconsin Department of Natural Resources, has resulted in the following listing:

Northwest Alabama State Junior College
Phil Campbell, Alabama 35581

Sheldon Jackson College
P.O. Box 479
Sitka, Alaska 99835

Red River Vocational-Technical School
P.O. Box E
Hope, Arkansas 71801

College of Redwoods
Eureka, California 95501

Los Angeles Trade-Technical College
450 North Grand Avenue
Los Angeles, California 90017

Porterville College
P.O. Box 952
Porterville, California 93257

Reedley College
995 North Reed Avenue
Reedley, California 93654

Sierra College
5000 Rocklin Road
Rocklin, California 95677

Santa Rosa Junior College
1501 Mendocino Avenue
Santa Rosa, California 95401

San Joaquin Delta College
3301 Kensington Way
Stockton, California 95204

Lassen Community College
1100 Main Street
Susanville, California 96130

Lake City Junior College
Route 1, Box 45
Lake City, Florida 32055

Savannah Area Vocational-Technical School
2001 Cynthia Street
Savannah, Georgia 31401

Abraham Baldwin Agricultural College
ABAC Station
Tifton, Georgia 31794

Waycross–Ware County Area Vocational Technical School
1701 Carswell Avenue
Waycross, Georgia 31501

North Idaho Junior College
1000 Garden Avenue
Coeur d'Alene, Idaho 83814

Southern Illinois University
Vocational-Technical Institute
Carbondale, Illinois 62901

Southeastern Illinois College
333 West College Street
Harrisburg, Illinois 62946

Haskell Institute
Bureau of Indian Affairs
U.S. Department of the Interior
Lawrence, Kansas 66044
(strongly recommended for Indian readers)

University of Kentucky
Forestry and Wood Technician School
Quicksand, Kentucky 41313

University of Maine
College of Life Sciences and Agriculture
Orono, Maine 04473

Unity College
Department of Forest Sciences
Unity, Maine 04988

Allegheny Community College
P.O. Box 870
Cumberland, Maryland 21502

Alpena Community College
Alpena, Michigan 21502

Michigan Technical University
Houghton, Michigan 49931

Ford Forestry Center
L'Anse, Michigan 49946

Brainerd Area Vocational Technical Institute
300 Quince Street
Brainerd, Minnesota 56401

Vermilion State Junior College
1900 East Camp Street
Ely, Minnesota 55731

Itasca State Junior College
Route 3
Grand Rapids, Minnesota 55744

North Central School
University of Minnesota
Grand Rapids, Minnesota 65744

Jones Junior College
Ellisville, Mississippi 39437

Southwest Missouri State College
901 South National Avenue
Springfield, Missouri 65802

Flathead Valley Community College
P.O. Box 1174
Kalispell, Montana 59901

Missoula Technical Center
909 South Avenue West
Missoula, Montana 59801

University of New Hampshire
Thompson School of Applied Sciences
Durham, New Hampshire 03824

State University of New York
Agricultural and Technical College
Morrisville, New York 13408

Paul Smith's College of Arts and Sciences
Paul Smiths, New York 12970

New York State Ranger School
Wanakena, New York 13695
(a college of environmental science and forestry)

Haywood Technical Institute
P.O. Box 457
Clyde, North Carolina 28721

Wayne Community College
P.O. Drawer 1878
Goldsboro, North Carolina 27530

Catawba Valley Technical Institute
Hickory, North Carolina 28601

Martin Technical Institute
P.O. Drawer 866
Williamston, North Carolina 27892

Hocking Technical College
Nelsonville, Ohio 45764

Northwestern State College
Industrial Education Department
Alva, Oklahoma 73717

Eastern Oklahoma State College
Wilburton, Oklahoma 74578

Clatsop Community College
16th and Jerome Avenue
Astoria, Oregon 97103

Central Oregon Community College
College Way
Bend, Oregon 97701

Southwestern Oregon Community College
Coos Bay, Oregon 97420

Lane Community College
4000 East 30th Avenue
Eugene, Oregon 97405

Mount Hood Community College
Gresham, Oregon 97030

Treasure Valley Community College
650 College Boulevard
Ontario, Oregon 97914

Umqua Community College
Roseburg, Oregon 97420

Chemeketa Community College
Salem, Oregon 97303

Salem Technical-Vocational Community College
Salem, Oregon 97402

The Pennsylvania State University
Mont Alto Campus
Mont Alto, Pennsylvania 17237

Williamsport Area Community College
1005 West Third Street
Williamsport, Pennsylvania 17701

Harry-Marion-Georgetown Technical
P.O. Box 317
Conway, South Carolina 29526

Dabney S. Lancaster Community College
Clifton Forge, Virginia 24422

Green River Community College
12401 S.E. 320th Street
Auburn, Washington 98002

Centralia College
P.O. Box 639
Centralia, Washington 98531

Everett Community College
801 Wetmore Avenue
Everett, Washington 98201

Peninsula College
Port Angeles, Washington 98362

Shoreline Community College
16101 Greenwood Avenue North
Seattle, Washington 98133

Spokane Falls Community College
W3410 Fort George Wright Drive
Spokane, Washington 99204

Wenatchee Valley College
Wenatchee, Washington 98801

Glenville State College
Glenville, West Virginia 26351

Fox Valley Technical Institute
1825 North Bluemound Drive
Appleton, Wisconsin 54911

Oshkosh Technical Institute
Oshkosh, Wisconsin 54901

Nicolet College
Rhinelander, Wisconsin 54501

Appendix B

COLLEGES AND UNIVERSITIES WITH ACADEMIC PROGRAMS LEADING TO PROFESSIONS IN THE CONSERVATION FIELD

Alabama	*Alabama Polytechnic Institute, Auburn 36830* *Auburn University, Auburn 36830*
Alaska	*University of Alaska, College 99701*
Arizona	*University of Arizona, Tucson 85721* *Northern Arizona University, Flagstaff 86003*

Arkansas	*Arkansas A & M College, College Heights*
	  71633
	University of Arkansas at Monticello,
	  Monticello 71655

British Columbia	*University of British Columbia, Vancouver,* *B.C., Canada*

California	*University of California, Berkeley 94720* *University of California, Davis 95616* *University of California, Los Angeles 90000* *Humboldt State College, Arcata 95521* *California State Polytechnic College, San Luis* *Obispo 93401*
Colorado	*Colorado State University, Fort Collins 80521*
Connecticut	*University of Connecticut, Storrs 06268* *Yale University, New Haven 06511*
Florida	*University of Florida, Gainesville 32601*
Georgia	*University of Georgia, Athens 30601*
Idaho	*University of Idaho, Moscow 83843*
Illinois	*University of Illinois, Urbana 61803* *Southern Illinois University, Carbondale 62903* *Northern Illinois University, De Kalb 60115* *Western Illinois University, Macomb 61455*
Indiana	*Purdue University, Lafayette 47907*
Iowa	*Iowa State University, Ames 50010*
Kansas	*University of Kansas, Lawrence 50707*
Kentucky	*University of Kentucky, Lexington 40506*
Louisiana	*Louisiana State University, Baton Rouge* *70803* *Louisiana Polytechnic Institute, Ruston 71270* *McNeese State College, Lake Charles 70601* *Louisiana Tech University, Ruston 71270*
Maine	*University of Maine, Orono 04473*
Massachusetts	*University of Massachusetts, Amherst 01003* *Harvard University, Petersham 01366*
Michigan	*Michigan State University, East Lansing* *48823* *University of Michigan, Ann Arbor 48104* *Michigan College of Mining and Technology,* *Houghton 49931*

	Lake Superior State College, Sault Sainte Marie 49783
Minnesota	*University of Minnesota, Saint Paul 55101*
Mississippi	*Mississippi State University, State College 39762*
Missouri	*University of Missouri, Columbia 65201*
Montana	*University of Montana, Missoula 59801* *Montana State University, Bozeman 59715*
Nebraska	*University of Nebraska, Lincoln 68500*
Nevada	*University of Nevada, Reno 89500*
New Hampshire	*University of New Hampshire, Durham 03824*
New Jersey	*Rutgers University, New Brunswick 08900*
New York	*Syracuse University, Syracuse 13210* *Cornell University, Ithaca 14850*
North Carolina	*North Carolina State University, Raleigh 27607* *Duke University, Durham 27706*
Ohio	*Ohio State University, Columbus 43200*
Oklahoma	*Oklahoma State University College, Stillwater 74075* *University of Oklahoma, Norman 73069*
Ontario	*Ontario Agricultural College, Guelph, Ontario, Canada* *University of Toronto, Toronto, Ontario, Canada*
Oregon	*Oregon State University, Corvallis 97331*
Pennsylvania	*Pennsylvania State University, Uuniversity Park 16802* *Pennsylvania State University, Mont Alto 17237*
Rhode Island	*University of Rhode Island, Kingston 02881*
South Carolina	*Clemson University, Clemson 29631*

South Dakota	*South Dakota State College, Brookings 57006*
Tennessee	*University of the South, Sewanee 37375* *University of Tennessee, Knoxville 37916*
Texas	*University of Texas, Austin 78700* *Stephen F. Austin State College, Nacogdoches 75962* *Texas A & M University, College Station 77843*
Utah	*Utah State University, Logan 84321*
Vermont	*University of Vermont, Burlington 05401*
Virginia	*Virginia Polytechnic Institute, Blacksburg 24061*
Washington	*University of Washington, Seattle 98105* *Washington State University, Pullman 99163* *Everett Community College, Everett 98201*
West Virginia	*West Virginia University, Morgantown 26506*
Wisconsin	*University of Wisconsin, Madison 53706* *University of Wisconsin, Milwaukee 53211* *Wisconsin State University, Stevens Point 54481*
Wyoming	*University of Wyoming, Laramie 82070*

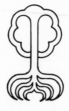

Appendix C

LEADING ACCREDITED SCHOOLS OF ENGINEERING

University of Alabama
University of Arizona
California Institute of Technology
University of California
Carnegie-Mellon University
Case Western Reserve University
University of Cincinnati
University of Colorado
Columbia University
Cornell University
Georgia Institute of Technology
Harvard University
University of Idaho
Illinois Institute of Technology
University of Illinois
Iowa State University of Science and Technology

University of Kansas
Lehigh University
Louisiana State University
Massachusetts Institute of Technology
Michigan Technological University
University of Michigan
University of Minnesota
University of Missouri
Montana State University
University of Nebraska
New York University
North Carolina Agricultural and Technical State University
University of North Dakota
Northwestern University, Illinois
University of Notre Dame, Indiana
Ohio State University
University of Oklahoma
Oregon State University
Pennsylvania State University
University of Pennsylvania
University of Pittsburgh
Princeton University
Purdue University
Rensselaer Polytechnic Institute
Rutgers University
South Dakota School of Mines and Technology
Stanford University
Stevens Institute of Technology, New Jersey
Syracuse University
University of Tennessee
Texas Agricultural and Mechanical University
University of Texas
University of Utah
Virginia Polytechnic Institute
Washington State University
University of Washington, Seattle
Washington University, Missouri
Wayne State University, Michigan
West Virginia University
University of Wisconsin
Yale University

Appendix D
GOVERNMENT PAY SCALES AND AGENCIES

AGENCIES

Forest Service
U.S. Department of Agriculture
Washington, D.C. 20250

NATIONAL FORESTS

Northern Region
Federal Building
Missoula, Montana 59801

IDAHO

    Clearwater, Orofino
    Coeur d'Alene, Coeur d'Alene
    Kaniksu, Sandpoint
    Nezperce, Grangeville
    St. Joe, Saint Maries

PAY SCALES (Effective October 19, 1974)

STEP	1	2	3	4	5	6	7	8	9	10
GS										
1	$ 5294	5470	5646	5822	5998	6174	6350	6526	6702	6878
2	5996	6196	6396	6596	6796	6996	7196	7396	7596	7796
3	6764	6989	7214	7439	7664	7889	8114	8339	8564	8789
4	7596	7849	8102	8355	8608	8861	9114	9367	9620	9873
5	8500	8783	9066	9349	9632	9915	10198	10481	10764	11047
6	9473	9789	10105	10421	10737	11053	11369	11685	12001	12317
7	10520	10871	11222	11573	11924	12275	12626	12977	13328	13679
8	11640	12028	12416	12804	13192	13580	13968	14356	14744	15132
9	12841	13269	13697	14125	14553	14981	15409	15837	16265	16693
10	14117	14588	15059	15530	16001	16472	16943	17414	17885	18356
11	15481	15997	16513	17029	17545	18061	18577	19093	19609	20125
12	18463	19078	19693	20308	20923	21538	22153	22768	23383	23998
13	21816	22543	23270	23997	24724	25451	26178	26905	27632	28359
14	25581	26434	27287	28140	28993	29846	30699	31552	32405	33258
15	25581	26434	27287	28140	28993	29846	30699	31552	32405	33258
16	34607	35761	36915*	38069*	39223*	40377*	41531*	42685*	43839*	
17	40062*	41397*	42732*	44067*	45402*					
18	46336*									

Waiting period for within-grade increases: to steps 2, 3, and 4–52 weeks; to steps 5, 6, and 7–104 weeks; to steps 8, 9, and 10–156 weeks.

* Actual rates for these steps, plus top four steps of GS-17 (not shown) held to $36,000 by law.

195

MONTANA
Beaverhead, Dillon
Bitterroot, Hamilton
Custer, Billings
Deerlodge, Butte
Flathead, Kalispell
Gallatin, Bozeman
Helena, Helena
Kootenai, Libby
Lewis and Clark, Great Falls
Lolo, Missoula

WASHINGTON
Colville, Colville

Rocky Mountain Region
Denver Federal Center, Building 85
Denver, Colorado 80225

COLORADO
Arapaho, Golden
Grand Mesa-Uncompahgre, Delta
Gunnison, Gunnison
Pike, Colorado Springs
Rio Grande, Monte Vista
Roosevelt, Fort Collins
Routt, Steamboat Springs
San Isabel, Pueblo
San Juan, Durango
White River, Glenwood Springs

NEBRASKA
Nebraska, Chadron

SOUTH DAKOTA
Black Hills, Custer

WYOMING
Bighorn, Sheridan
Medicine Bow, Laramie
Shoshone, Cody

Southwestern Region
517 Gold Avenue S.W.
Albuquerque, New Mexico 87101

ARIZONA
Apache, Springerville
Coconino, Flagstaff
Coronado, Tucson
Kaibab, Williams
Prescott, Prescott
Sitgreaves, Holbrook
Tonto, Phoenix

NEW MEXICO
Carson, Taos
Cibola, Albuquerque
Gila, Silver City
Lincoln, Alamogordo
Santa Fe, Santa Fe

Intermountain Region
324 25th Street
Ogden, Utah 84401

IDAHO
Boise, Boise
Caribou, Pocatello
Challis, Challis
Payette, McCall
Salmon, Salmon
Sawtooth, Twin Falls
Targhee, Saint Anthony

NEVADA
Humboldt, Elko
Toiyabe, Reno

UTAH
Ashley, Vernal
Cache, Logan
Dixie, Cedar City
Fishlake, Richfield

Manti-La Sal, Price
Uinta, Provo
Wasatch, Salt Lake City

WYOMING
Bridger, Kemmerer
Teton, Jackson

California Region
630 Sansome Street
San Francisco, California 94111

CALIFORNIA
Angeles, Pasadena
Cleveland, San Diego
Eldorado, Placerville
Inyo, Bishop
Klamath, Yreka
Lassen, Susanville
Los Padres, Santa Barbara
Mendocino, Willows
Modoc, Alturas
Plumas, Quincy
San Bernardino, San Bernardino
Sequoia, Porterville
Shasta-Trinity, Redding
Sierra, Fresno
Six Rivers, Eureka
Stanislaus, Sonora
Tahoe, Nevada City

Pacific Northwest Region
319 S.W. Pine Street
P.O. Box 3623
Portland, Oregon 97208

OREGON
Deshutes, Bend
Fremont, Lakeview
Malheur, John Day
Mount Hood, Portland

Ochoco, Prineville
Rogue River, Medford
Siskiyou, Grants Pass
Siuslaw, Corvallis
Umatilla, Pendleton
Umpqua, Roseburg
Wallowa-Whitman, Baker
Willamette, Eugene
Winema, Klamath Falls

WASHINGTON
Gifford Pinchot, Vancouver
Mount Baker, Bellingham
Okanogan, Okanogan
Olympic, Olympia
Snoqualmie, Seattle
Wenatchee, Wenatchee

Eastern Region
633 West Wisconsin Avenue
Milwaukee, Wisconsin 53203

ILLINOIS
Shawnee, Harrisburg

INDIANA
Hoosier, Bedford

MICHIGAN
Hiawatha, Escanaba
Huron, Cadillac
Manistee, Cadillac
Ottawa, Ironwood

MINNESOTA
Chippewa, Cass Lake
Superior, Duluth

MISSOURI
Clark, Rolla
Mark Twain, Rolla
(these two now combined and called National Forests in
Missouri)

NEW HAMPSHIRE
White Mountain, Laconia

OHIO
Wayne, Bedford, Indiana

PENNSYLVANIA
Allegheny, Warren

VERMONT
Green Mountain, Rutland

WEST VIRGINIA
Monongahela, Elkins

WISCONSIN
Chequamegon, Park Falls
Nicolet, Rhinelander

Southern Region
1720 Peachtree Road N.W.
Atlanta, Georgia 30309

ALABAMA
William B. Bankhead
Conecuh
Talladega
Tuskegee

Address *National Forests in Alabama*
1765 Highland Avenue
P.O. Box 40
Montgomery 36101

ARKANSAS
Ouachita, Hot Springs
Ozark, Russellville
Saint Francis, Russellville

FLORIDA
Apalachicola
Ocala
Osceola

Address *National Forests in Florida*
214 South Bronough Street
P.O. Box 1050
Tallahassee 32302

GEORGIA
    Chattahoochee
    Oconee

Address *National Forests in Georgia*
322 Oak Street N.W.
Gainesville 30501

KENTUCKY
    Daniel Boone, Winchester

LOUISIANA
    Kisatche, Pineville

MISSISSIPPI
    Bienville
    Delta
    DeSoto
    Holly Springs
    Homochitto
    Tombigbee

Address *National Forests in Mississippi*
350 Milner Building
P.O. Box 1291
Jackson 39205

NORTH CAROLINA
    Croatan
    Nantahala
    Pisgah
    Uwharrie

Address *National Forests in North Carolina*
B-level Plateau Building
50 South French Broad
P.O. Box 2570
Asheville 28802

SOUTH CAROLINA
    Francis Marion
    Sumter

Address *National Forests in South Carolina*
Room 350
1801 Main Street
Columbia 29201

TENNESSEE
    Cherokee, Cleveland

TEXAS
    Angelina
    Davy Crockett
    Sabine
    Sam Houston

Address *National Forests in Texas*
Federal Building
P.O. Box 969
Lufkin 75901

VIRGINIA
    George Washington, Harrisonburg
    Jefferson, Roanoke

Alaska Region
Federal Office Building
P.O. Box 1628
Juneau, Alaska 99801

ALASKA
    Chugach, Anchorage
    North Tongass, Juneau
    South Tongass, Ketchikan

RESEARCH HEADQUARTERS

Forest Products Laboratory
North Walnut Street
P.O. Box 5130
Madison, Wisconsin 53705

Institute of Tropical Forestry
P.O. Box AQ
Rio Piedras, Puerto Rico 00928

Institute of Northern Forestry
Fairbanks, Alaska 99701

FOREST AND RANGE EXPERIMENT STATIONS

Pacific Northwest
809 N.E. Sixth Avenue
P.O. Box 3141
Portland, Oregon 97208

Pacific Southwest
1960 Addison Street
Berkeley, California 94701

Intermountain
507 25th Street
Ogden, Utah 84401

Rocky Mountain
240 West Prospect Street
Fort Collins, Colorado 80521

North Central
Folwell Avenue
Saint Paul, Minnesota 55101

Northeastern
6816 Market Street
Upper Darby, Pennsylvania 19082

Southern
Federal Building
701 Loyola Avenue
New Orleans, Louisiana 70113

Southeastern
Post Office Building
P.O. Box 2570
Asheville, North Carolina 28802

NOTE: There are state and private forestry areas headquartered at Upper Darby, Pennsylvania, and Atlanta, Georgia, and national grasslands in the Northern, Rocky Mountain, and Southwestern Regions.

Tennessee Valley Authority
New Sprankle Building
Knoxville, Tennessee 37902

The TVA, a quasi-federal organization, has its own separate recruitment policy, pay scales (described in the text), retirement policy, etc. The TVA has employment branch offices at Chattanooga, Knoxville, and Nashville, Tennessee, and Muscle Shoals, Alabama, and at each major construction project. You can get an application form if you write or come to one of these offices. Applications are accepted at any time. Personal interviews are desirable, though not necessary. To become eligible for some jobs you have to take tests, but this does not apply to most outdoor jobs. Age range is sixteen to seventy. Write to the above address for more information.

Soil Conservation Service
Washington, D.C. 20250

Below are listed the regional biologists and recreation specialists associated with the SCS. In addition, each state has field biologists and conservationists.

REGIONAL BIOLOGISTS

NORTHEAST
Carl H. Thomas
7600 West Chester Pike
Upper Darby, Pennsylvania 19082

SOUTH
Olan W. Dillon, Jr.
P.O. Box 11222
3600 McCart Street
Fort Worth, Texas 76110

MIDWEST
Wade H. Hamor
Room 503
134 South 12th Street
Lincoln, Nebraska 68508

WEST

L. Dean Marriage
Federal Building
511 N.W. Broadway
Portland, Oregon 97209

REGIONAL RECREATION SPECIALISTS

EAST

Hans G. Uhlig
7600 West Chester Pike
Upper Darby, Pennsylvania 19082

SOUTH

Ross J. Miller
P.O. Box 11222
3600 McCart Street
Fort Worth, Texas 76110

MIDWEST

C. V. Bohart
134 South 12th Street
Lincoln, Nebraska 68508

WEST

Charles Maesner
Ross Building
209 S.W. 5th Avenue
Portland, Oregon 97204

U.S. Army Corps of Engineers
Office of the Chief of Engineers
Forrestal Building
Washington, D.C. 20314

DIVISION AND DISTRICT OFFICES

NEW ENGLAND DIVISION

Division Engineer
U.S. Army Engineer Division
New England
424 Trapelo Road
Waltham, Massachusetts 02154

NORTH ATLANTIC DIVISION

Division Engineer
U.S. Army Engineer Division
North Atlantic
90 Church Street
New York, New York 10007

District Engineer
U.S. Army Engineer District
Baltimore
31 Hopkins Plaza
P.O. Box 1715
Baltimore, Maryland 21203

District Engineer
U.S. Army Engineer District
Norfolk
803 Front Street
Norfolk, Virginia 23510

District Engineer
U.S. Army Engineer District
New York
26 Federal Plaza
New York, New York 10007

District Engineer
U.S. Army Engineer District
Philadelphia
U.S. Custom House
2nd and Chestnut Streets
Philadelphia, Pennsylvania 19106

SOUTH ATLANTIC DIVISION

Division Engineer
U.S. Army Engineer Division
South Atlantic
510 Title Building
30 Pryor Street S.W.
Atlanta, Georgia 30303

District Engineer
U.S. Army Engineer District
Charleston
Federal Building
334 Meeting Street
P.O. Box 919
Charleston, South Carolina 29402

District Engineer
U.S. Army Engineer District
Savannah
200 East St. Julian Street
P.O. Box 889
Savannah, Georgia 31402

District Engineer
U.S. Army Engineer District
Wilmington
308 Federal Building
P.O. Box 1890
Wilmington, North Carolina 28401

District Engineer
U.S. Army Engineer District
Mobile
2301 Airport Boulevard
Mobile, Alabama 36601

District Engineer
U.S. Army Engineer District
Jacksonville
400 West Bay Street
P.O. Box 4970
Jacksonville, Florida 32201

OHIO RIVER DIVISION
   Division Engineer
   U.S. Army Engineer Division
   Ohio River
   550 Main Street
   P.O. Box 1159
   Cincinnati, Ohio 45201

District Engineer
U.S. Army Engineer District
Huntington
502 Eighth Street
P.O. Box 2127
Huntington, West Virginia 25721

District Engineer
U.S. Army Engineer District
Louisville
600 Federal Plaza
P.O. Box 59
Louisville, Kentucky 40201

District Engineer
U.S. Army Engineer District
Nashville
306 Federal Office Building
P.O. Box 1070
Nashville, Tennessee 37202

District Engineer
U.S. Army Engineer District
Pittsburgh
Federal Building
1000 Liberty Avenue
Pittsburgh, Pennsylvania 15222

NORTH CENTRAL DIVISION
Division Engineer
U.S. Army Engineer Division
North Central
536 South Clark Street
Chicago, Illinois 60605

District Engineer
U.S. Army Engineer District
Buffalo
1776 Niagara Street
Buffalo, New York 14207

District Engineer
U.S. Army Engineer District

Rock Island
Clock Tower Building
Rock Island, Illinois 61201

District Engineer
U.S. Army Engineer District
Chicago
219 South Dearborn Street
Chicago, Illinois 60604

District Engineer
U.S. Army Engineer District
Saint Paul
1210 U.S. Post Office and Customhouse
Saint Paul, Minnesota 55101

District Engineer
U.S. Army Engineer District
Detroit
150 Michigan Avenue
P.O. Box 1027
Detroit, Michigan 48231

LOWER MISSISSIPPI VALLEY DIVISION
Division Engineer
U.S. Army Engineer Division
Lower Mississippi Valley
Walnut and Crawford Streets
P.O. Box 80
Vicksburg, Mississippi 39182

District Engineer
U.S. Army Engineer District
Memphis
668 Federal Office Building
Memphis, Tennessee 38103

District Engineer
U.S. Army Engineer District
New Orleans
Foot of Prytania Street
P.O. Box 60267
New Orleans, Louisiana 70160

District Engineer
U.S. Army Engineer District
Saint Louis
210 North 12th Street
Saint Louis, Missouri 63101

District Engineer
U.S. Army Engineer District
Vicksburg
U.S. Post Office and Courthouse Building
P.O. Box 60
Vicksburg, Mississippi 39180

MISSOURI RIVER DIVISION
Division Engineer
U.S. Army Engineer Division
Missouri River
U.S. Post Office and Courthouse
215 North 17th Street
P.O. Box 103 (Downtown Station)
Omaha, Nebraska 68101

District Engineer
U.S. Army Engineer District
Kansas City
700 Federal Office Building
601 East 12th Street
Kansas City, Missouri 64106

District Engineer
U.S. Army Engineer District
Omaha
7410 U.S. Post Office and Courthouse
215 North 17th Street
Omaha, Nebraska 68102

SOUTHWESTERN DIVISION
Division Engineer
U.S. Army Engineer Division
Southwestern
1114 Commerce Street
Dallas, Texas 75202

District Engineer
U.S. Army Engineer District
Albuquerque
517 Gold Avenue S.W.
P.O. Box 1580
Albuquerque, New Mexico 87103

District Engineer
U.S. Army Engineer District
Little Rock
700 West Capitol
P.O. Box 867
Little Rock, Arkansas 72203

District Engineer
U.S. Army Engineer District
Fort Worth
819 Taylor Street
P.O. Box 17300
Fort Worth, Texas 76102

District Engineer
U.S. Army Engineer District
Tulsa
224 South Boulder
P.O. Box 61
Tulsa, Oklahoma 74102

District Engineer
U.S. Army Engineer District
Galveston
Santa Fe Building
P.O. Box 1229
Galveston, Texas 77550

NORTH PACIFIC DIVISION
Division Engineer
U.S. Army Engineer Division
North Pacific
220 N.W. 8th Avenue
Portland, Oregon 97209

District Engineer
U.S. Army Engineer District
Alaska
P.O. Box 7002
Anchorage, Alaska 99501

District Engineer
U.S. Army Engineer District
Portland
2850 S.E. 82nd Avenue
P.O. Box 2946
Portland, Oregon 97208

District Engineer
U.S. Army Engineer District
Seattle
1519 Alaskan Way, South
Seattle, Washington 98134

District Engineer
U.S. Army Engineer District
Walla Walla
Building 602
City-County Airport
Walla Walla, Washington 99362

SOUTH PACIFIC DIVISION

Division Engineer
U.S. Army Engineer Division
South Pacific
630 Sansome Street, Room 1216
San Francisco, California 94111

District Engineer
U.S. Army Engineer District
Los Angeles
300 North Los Angeles Street
P.O. Box 2711
Los Angeles, California 90053

District Engineer
U.S. Army Engineer District

San Francisco
100 McAllister Street
San Francisco, California 94102

District Engineer
U.S. Army Engineer District
Sacramento
650 Capitol Mall
Sacramento, California 95814

PACIFIC OCEAN DIVISION
Division Engineer
U.S. Army Engineer Division
Pacific Ocean
Building 96, Fort Armstrong
Honolulu, Hawaii 96813

Bureau of Land Management
Washington, D.C. 20240

In addition to the two BLM service centers listed below, each of the western states has a state director.

DENVER SERVICE CENTER
Serves Arizona, Colorado, Montana, New Mexico, Utah, and Wyoming.

Director
Garth H. Rudd
Denver Federal Center
Building 50
Denver, Colorado 80225

PORTLAND SERVICE CENTER
Serves Alaska, California, Idaho, Nevada, Oregon, and Washington.

Director
Edward G. Bygland
710 N.E. Holladay Street
Box 3861
Portland, Oregon 97208

Bureau of Outdoor Recreation
Washington, D.C. 20240

The seven regional offices are listed below. In addition, there are state liaison officers in each state.

REGIONAL OFFICES

NORTHEAST

Regional Director Bureau of Outdoor Recreation
Federal Building, 7th Floor
1421 Cherry Street
Philadelphia, Pennsylvania 19102

SOUTHEAST

Regional Director Bureau of Outdoor Recreation
810 New Walton Building
Atlanta, Georgia 30303

LAKE CENTRAL

Regional Director Bureau of Outdoor Recreation
3853 Research Park Drive
Ann Arbor, Michigan 48104

MID-CONTINENT

Regional Director Bureau of Outdoor Recreation
41 Denver Federal Center
Denver, Colorado 80225

NORTHWEST

Regional Director Bureau of Outdoor Recreation
1000 Second Avenue
Seattle, Washington 98104

PACIFIC SOUTHWEST

Regional Director Bureau of Outdoor Recreation
Box 36062
450 Golden Gate Avenue
San Francisco, California 94102

SOUTH CENTRAL

Regional Director Bureau of Outdoor Recreation
5301 Central Avenue N.E.
Albuquerque, New Mexico 87108

Bureau of Reclamation
Washington, D.C. 20240

PACIFIC NORTHWEST REGION
Regional Director
P.O. Box 043
U.S. Court House
550 West Fort Street
Boise, Idaho 83702

MID-PACIFIC REGION
Regional Director
Federal Office Building
2800 Cottage Way
Sacramento, California 95825

LOWER COLORADO REGION
Regional Director
P.O. Box 427
Boulder City, Nevada 89005

UPPER COLORADO REGION
Regional Director
P.O. Box 11568
Salt Lake City, Utah 84111

SOUTHWEST REGION
Regional Director
Herring Plaza
Box H-4377
Amarillo, Texas 79101

UPPER MISSOURI REGION
Regional Director
Box 2553
Billings, Montana 59103

LOWER MISSOURI REGION
Regional Director
Building 20, Denver Federal Center
Denver, Colorado 80225

Fish and Wildlife Service
Washington, D.C. 20240

In addition to the seven regional headquarters listed below, there are wildlife research laboratories and sport fisheries research laboratories in various parts of the country.

PACIFIC REGION
Regional Director
1500 Plaza Building
1500 N.E. Irving Street
Portland, Oregon 97208

SOUTHWEST REGION
Regional Director
Federal Building
U.S. Post Office and Court House
500 Gold Avenue S.W.
Albuquerque, New Mexico 87103

NORTH CENTRAL REGION
Regional Director
Federal Building
Fort Snelling
Twin Cities, Minnesota 55111

SOUTHEAST REGION
Regional Director
Peachtree Street, 7th Building
Atlanta, Georgia 30323

NORTHEAST REGION
Regional Director
U.S. Post Office and Courthouse
Boston, Massachusetts 02109

ALASKA AREA
Regional Director
6917 Seward Highway
Anchorage, Alaska 99502

DENVER REGION
Regional Director
10597 West 6th Avenue
Denver, Colorado 80215

Geological Survey
GSA Building
Washington, D.C. 20242

EASTERN REGION
Assistant Director
Mail Stop 171, Geological Survey National Center
Reston, Virginia 22092

CENTRAL REGION
Assistant Director
Federal Center, Building 25
Denver, Colorado 80225

WESTERN REGION
Assistant Director
345 Middlefield Road
Menlo Park, California 94025

National Park Service
Interior Building
Washington, D.C. 20240

NORTHEAST REGION
Regional Director
143 South Third Street
Philadelphia, Pennsylvania 19106

SOUTHEAST REGION
Regional Director
3401 Whipple Avenue
Atlanta, Georgia 30344

SOUTHWEST REGION
Regional Director
Old Santa Fe Trail
P.O. Box 728
Santa Fe, New Mexico 87501

MIDWEST REGION
Regional Director
1709 Jackson Street
Omaha, Nebraska 68102

WESTERN REGION
Regional Director
450 Golden Gate Avenue
P.O. Box 36063
San Francisco, California 94102

PACIFIC NORTHWEST REGION
Regional Director
1424 Fourth Avenue
Seattle, Washington 98101

NATIONAL CAPITAL PARKS
Director
1100 Ohio Drive S.W.
Washington, D.C. 20242

Environmental Protection Agency
U.S. Waterside Mall
Washington, D.C. 20460

EPA has ten regions, in Boston, Maine; New York, New York; Philadelphia, Pennsylvania; Atlanta, Georgia; Chicago, Illinois; Dallas, Texas; Kansas City, Missouri; Denver, Colorado; San Francisco, California; and Seattle, Washington.

Appendix E

APPLYING FOR CIVIL SERVICE JOBS

Under the Civil Service merit system, appointments to jobs are made on the basis of ability to do the work—ability demonstrated in competition with other applicants. All qualified applicants receive consideration for appointment without regard to race, religion, color, national origin, sex, politics, or any other nonmerit factor.

The examining system functions through sixty-five area offices of the Civil Service Commission, located in centers of population throughout the country. There is at least one in every state.

These area offices announce and conduct examinations. They check applicants' work experience, training, and aptitude. They send the names of people who meet the requirements to federal agencies who are seeking new employees. Each office also provides, through its Federal Job Information Center, a complete one-stop information service about federal job opportunities in the area as well as in other locations. Many post offices also furnish information about current job opportunities and give out application forms.

Before you apply for a job, read the announcement carefully. It gives information about the job to be filled and what qualifications you must have to fill it. Don't waste your time or that of the government by applying for jobs you are not qualified for. But don't be backward, either, in applying for those you think you are qualified for, and be sure to fill out the application completely, listing all your experience, no matter how trivial it may seem to you. You want the highest rating possible, and your rating may depend on details you think are unimportant.

Here are addresses of Federal Job Information Centers:

ALABAMA

Southerland Building
806 Governors Drive S.W.
Huntsville 35801

107 Saint Francis Street
Mobile 36602

ALASKA

Hill Building
632 6th Avenue
Anchorage 99051

Suite 7, Rampart Building
529 5th Avenue
Fairbanks 99701

ARIZONA

Balke Building
44 West Adams Street
Phoenix 85003

ARKANSAS

Room 1319
Federal Office Building
700 West Capital Avenue
Little Rock 72201

CALIFORNIA
> 1340 Pine Avenue
> Long Beach 90813
>
> 851 South Broadway
> Los Angeles 90014
>
> Room 207
> Post Office Building
> 120 West Cypress Street
> Santa Maria 93454
>
> Room 4210
> 650 Capitol Mall
> Sacramento 95814
>
> 1400 5th Avenue, Suite 100
> San Diego 92101
>
> 450 Golden Gate Avenue
> San Francisco 94102

COLORADO
> Room 203, Post Office Building
> 1823 Stout Street
> Denver 80202

CONNECTICUT
> Room 716, Federal Building
> 450 Main Street
> Hartford 06103

DELAWARE
> Post Office and Courthouse
> 11th and King Streets
> Wilmington 19801

FLORIDA
> 3101 Maguire Boulevard
> Orlando 32803

GEORGIA
> 275 Peachtree Street N.E.
> Atlanta 30303

Federal Building
451 College Street
Macon 31201

HAWAII
  Federal Building
  Honolulu 96813

IDAHO
  Room 663, Federal Building
  U.S. Courthouse
  550 West Fort Street
  Boise 83702

ILLINOIS
  Room 1322
  219 South Dearborn Street
  Chicago 60604

  Building 3400
  Electronics Supply Office
  Great Lakes 60088

  Building 103
  Rock Island Arsenal
  Rock Island 61201

INDIANA
  Room 102
  36 South Pennsylvania Street
  Indianapolis 46204

IOWA
  191 Federal Building
  210 Walnut Street
  Des Moines 50309

KANSAS
  Room 101, One-Twenty Building
  120 South Market Street
  Wichita 67202

KENTUCKY
   Room 167, Federal Building
   600 Federal Plaza
   Louisville 40202

LOUISIANA
   Federal Building South
   600 South Street
   New Orleans 70130

MAINE
   Federal Building
   Augusta 04330

MARYLAND
   Federal Office Building
   Lombard Street and Hopkins Place
   Baltimore 21201

MASSACHUSETTS
   Post Office and Courthouse Building
   Boston 02109

MICHIGAN
   Room 1026
   144 West Lafayette Street
   Detroit 48226

MINNESOTA
   Room 116, Federal Building
   Minneapolis 55401

MISSISSIPPI
   802 North State Street
   Jackson 39201

MISSOURI
   Federal Building, Room 129
   601 East 12th Street
   Kansas City 64106

Federal Building, Room 1712
1520 Market Street
Saint Louis 63103

MONTANA
I.B.M.
130 Neill Avenue
Helena 59601

NEBRASKA
Courthouse and Post Office Building
Room 102
215 North 17th Street
Omaha 68102

NEVADA
300 Booth Street
Reno 89502

300 Las Vegas Boulevard South
Las Vegas 89101

NEW HAMPSHIRE
Federal Building–U.S. Post Office
Daniel and Penhallow Streets
Portsmouth 03803

NEW JERSEY
Federal Building
970 Broad Street
Newark 07102

NEW MEXICO
Federal Building
421 Gold Avenue S.W.
Albuquerque 87101

NEW YORK
Federal Building
26 Federal Plaza
New York 10007

O'Donnell Building
301 Erie Boulevard West
Syracuse 13202

NORTH CAROLINA
310 New Bern Avenue
P.O. Box 25069
Raleigh 27611

NORTH DAKOTA
Room 20C, Federal Building and Post Office
657 Second Avenue North
Fargo 58102

OHIO
Room 1523
Federal Office Building
550 Main Street
Cincinnati 45202

New Federal Building
1240 East 9th Street
Cleveland 44199

Knott Building
21 East 4th Street
Dayton 45402

OKLAHOMA
210 N.W. 6th Street
Oklahoma City 73102

OREGON
319 S.W. Pine Street
Portland 97204

PENNSYLVANIA
Federal Building
128 North Broad Street
Philadelphia 19102

Federal Building
1000 Liberty Avenue
Pittsburgh 15222

RHODE ISLAND
Federal Building and Post Office
Kennedy Plaza
Providence 02903

SOUTH CAROLINA
Federal Office Building
334 Meeting Street
Charleston 29403

SOUTH DAKOTA
Dusek Building, Room 118
919 Main Street
Rapid City 57701

TENNESSEE
Federal Office Building
167 North Main Street
Memphis 38103

TEXAS
Downtown Postal Building
701 North Upper Broadway
Corpus Christi 78401

Room 1C42
1100 Commerce Street
Dallas 75202

El Paso National Bank Building
411 North Stanton Street
El Paso 79901

Room 1-F-00
819 Taylor Street
Fort Worth 76102

702 Caroline Street
Houston 77002

Post Office and Courthouse Building
615 East Houston Street
San Antonio 78205

UTAH

Federal Building Annex
135 South State Street
Salt Lake City 84111

VERMONT

Federal Building
Elmwood Avenue and Pearl Street
Burlington 05401

VIRGINIA

Rotunda Building
415 Saint Paul Boulevard
Norfolk 23510

WASHINGTON

511 Burwell Street
Bremerton 98314

Federal Office Building
1st Avenue and Madison Street
Seattle 98104

WEST VIRGINIA

Federal Building
500 Quarrier Street
Charleston 25301

WISCONSIN

Room 215
161 West Wisconsin Avenue
Milwaukee 53203

WYOMING

Room 108
1805 Capitol Avenue
Cheyenne 82001

WASHINGTON, D.C.
CSC Building
1900 E Street N.W.
Washington, D.C. 20415

PUERTO RICO AND THE VIRGIN ISLANDS
Pan Am Building
255 Ponce de Leon Avenue
San Juan 00917

INDEX